Palgrave Studies in Latin American Heterodox Economics

The aim of the series is to analyze the economic, social, and political evolution of countries in Latin America. The authors in the series are serious heterodox economics scholars who want to shine light on Latin America's economic profile. Each book in the series takes on a single topic (crisis, growth, income distribution, the manufacturing sector, etc.), either from the point of view of a single country or a group of them. This analysis then in turn adds to our understanding of Latin America's regional economic character and development challenges and capabilities. In this way, this series makes an unusual contribution to economics by studying a region as a whole without losing sight of the particularities of each country as a part.

All proposals submitted to the series undergo documented single-blind peer review by subject-matter experts (SME). In addition, all manuscripts are reviewed by SME prior to acceptance through a documented single-blind process.

Eva Paus • Rafael Domínguez

Toward Inclusive Development in Latin America

Leveraging the Global Green Transition

palgrave
macmillan

Eva Paus
Economics
Mount Holyoke College
South Hadley, MA, USA

Rafael Domínguez
Economics
Universidad de Cantabria
Santander, Cantabria, Spain

ISSN 2662-3943 ISSN 2662-3951 (electronic)
Palgrave Studies in Latin American Heterodox Economics
ISBN 978-3-032-08587-0 ISBN 978-3-032-08588-7 (eBook)
https://doi.org/10.1007/978-3-032-08588-7

This Palgrave Macmillan imprint is published by the registered company Springer Nature Switzerland AG.
The registered company address is: Gewerbestrasse 11, 6330 Cham, Switzerland

This book is dedicated to the prospect of inclusive development
for all Latin Americans

Preface and Acknowledgments

We have devoted our academic careers to researching economic development challenges and achievements in the Global South, often with a focus on Latin America. The idea for this book arose after we participated in a collaborative research project on natural resource extractivism in Latin America and the Maghreb at the University of Kassel, Germany.

We are grateful to Hans-Jürgen Burchardt and Hannes Warnecke-Berger, leaders of the Latin American part of the project, for offering us a month-long fellowship in the project in 2022 (Domínguez) and 2023 (Paus). The discussions with fellow researchers from Latin America and elsewhere, and with the participants in several related conferences, were stimulating and thought-provoking.

One of the hotly debated questions was whether the global green transition offers an opportunity for resource-rich Latin American countries to change the trajectory of their commodity-dependent economies. Previous opportunities, most recently the commodity super cycle of the 2000s, were generally not leveraged strategically to put economies on a path to sustained development. So, can this time be different? And if so, why and how?

The answers to these questions are particularly important since the economic challenges of low productivity and economic growth and limited social inclusion in the region have been growing. In this book, we analyze the conditions that can make this time different, the conditions under which the global green transition can lead to transformational change in Latin America's development. We argue that such a transformation requires a systemic approach to policymaking, with a green environmental state leading a strategy to increase social inclusion and productivity growth and reduce the use of fossil fuels. Based on an approach which integrates heterodox economics and international geopolitical economy, we analyze the opportunities and challenges offered at the current juncture for the adoption and implementation of an inclusive green development strategy. The scope of our analysis is broad, as are the general policy recommendations. Nonetheless, throughout, we highlight country heterogeneity in the region, and emphasize that the constellation of country-specific economic structures and political coalitions in support of inclusive green development will necessarily vary.

We wrote this book at a time of growing upheaval in the global economy, heightened geopolitical tensions, and huge uncertainty about the future. The hyper-globalization of the past decades has increased inequality between and in many countries around the world and led to rising discontent and a demand for new policies. Progressive governments can leverage this demand in support of an inclusive green transformation, but governments on the right can tap into it as well, though with different intentions. The rapid pace of technological change, especially advances in AI and robotics, is greatly contributing to the radical uncertainty about the future, due to its impact on the future of work and people's well-being. Add to this the vicissitudes of Trump Administration policies and their disregard for national and international norms and institutions, and you have extraordinary volatility and unpredictability, including the prospect of continuing progressive governments in Latin America.

Thus, we refrain from making any predictions, except for one. Regardless of what the future international order will turn out to be, in the absence of a systemic change in development strategy with a green developmental state at the core, the key development challenges in the region will intensify. For this book, we took account of the implications of policies and events until the middle of June 2025.

We are solely responsible for the content of this book. But in writing this book, we benefited from the insights of many colleagues and friends. We particularly thank Luis Abugattas, James Boyce, Gonzalo Hernandez, Mauricio León, and Michelle Viera Romero for thoughtful discussions on different issues in the book, Lisa Sachs for helpful comments on an early draft of the section on state-investor dispute settlement, and José Antonio Ocampo, Esteban Valenzuela, and José Miguel Ahumada for insightful interviews. Hannes Warnecke-Berger, Steve Ellner, Zirui Wu, and Daniel Morales resolved various doubts and offered some important documentation. Maira Khan and Ivy Tram provided excellent research assistance. Eva Paus thanks Barbara Fritz for hosting her at the Institute for Latin American Studies at the Free University of Berlin in the fall of 2024, which offered opportunities for productive discussions and writing.

Special thanks go to our families who supported us all the way.

South Hadley, MA, USA — Eva Paus
Santander, Spain — Rafael Domínguez

Competing Interests The authors have no competing interests to declare that are relevant to the content of this manuscript.

Praise for *Toward Inclusive Development in Latin America*

"*Toward Inclusive Development in Latin America* is a lucid, courageous, timely and well-documented contribution to the need for Latin America to create its specific path towards sustainable development departing from the continent's particular set of natural resources. The book uses political economy approaches which point to the need to create different political alliances that can put the state as a central agent for such a development. Very welcome, indeed."

—Luis Bértola, Professor of *Economic History and Development, Universidad de la República, Uruguay*

"Domínguez and Paus have put forth a twenty-first-century growth trajectory for Latin America that capitalizes on the region's location-specific assets in transition minerals, large endowments of solar and wind energy potential, and deep and underutilized store of human capital. The authors show how countries can engage in green structural transformation that can result in lower carbon, more socially inclusive, and resilient economic growth paths. Such a strategy will take a spark of political and economic investment. The costs of inaction on such a strategy far outweigh such investments, making this book an essential and urgent blueprint."

—Kevin Gallagher, Professor and Director, *Boston University Global Development Policy Center*

"This book is a major contribution to the analysis of how to fulfill the triple dimensions of sustainable development: economic growth, social development, and environmental sustainability. A 'green development state' at the center of an inclusive green development strategy, together with the promotion of regional cooperation, are essential proposals for both national development and the contribution of Latin America to the achievement of major global goals."

—José Antonio Ocampo, Professor, *Columbia University*, former Minister of Finance of Colombia and UN Under-Secretary-General for Economic and Social Affairs

"Using a combination of heterodox economics and international geopolitical economy Paus and Domínguez propose a timely and innovative strategy—Inclusive Green Development (IGD)—that Latin American countries should adopt to address three major obstacles to their social and economic progress: growth-reducing structural change, limited social inclusion and high inequalities, and climate change. Two fundamental pillars for its effective implementation are a green developmental state and a broad-based agreement on industrial policies. The development strategy and policy proposals outlined are not only applicable to the Latin American context but also highly relevant to the broader developing world."

—Esteban Pérez Caldentey, Chief of the Financing Unit for Development, Economic Development Division, Economic Commission for Latin America and the Caribbean (ECLAC)

"The climate transition poses a significant challenge to Latin America's development ambitions. This book shows how it can be turned into an opportunity. Paus and Domínguez make a timely and useful case for green industrial policies as the cornerstone of inclusive economic growth strategies in the region. Scholars and policy makers alike will benefit from their analysis."

—Dani Rodrik, Professor, *Harvard University*

"How can Latin American countries consolidate a greener, more equitable and more dynamic future? *Toward Inclusive Development in Latin America* calls for a new policy approach: green industrial policy together with a more redistributive state can deliver win-win-win solutions. The book offers a detailed discussion of the interventions required for structural transformation and green growth. Going beyond policy recommendations, it also considers the political economic conditions needed to deliver successful change. Internally, it calls for new state–society relations with a central role for the middle class and social movements. Externally, it proposes a non-alignment strategy in the current great power competition between the US and China. This superb book is a necessary read for students of Latin American development and policymakers alike."

—Diego Sánchez-Ancochea, Professor of the *Political Economy of Development, University of Oxford*

Contents

About the Authors

Rafael Domínguez is Professor of Economic History and Institutions in the Department of Economics at the University of Cantabria, Spain. He is a fellow of the Social Science Doctoral Program at the University of Salamanca, Spain. Domínguez leads the international research group on South-South Cooperation and Regional Integrations of the Spanish Network of Development Studies, and he has collaborated with CEPAL, GIZ, Europeaid, and the international development cooperation agencies of Mexico and Chile.

Eva Paus is Professor of Economics Emerita at Mount Holyoke College, USA, and non-resident senior fellow at the Global Development Policy Center at Boston University. Her recent research has focused on economic development in the context of globalization in the face of structural change, innovation, and the middle-income trap in Latin America and beyond. She is the author of several books, including *Global Capitalism Unbound, Confronting Dystopia, and Foreign Investment, Development, and Globalization*. Paus has collaborated with ECLAC, ILO, UNIDO, and UNDP.

Abbreviations

AI	Artificial intelligence
AIIB	Asian Infrastructure Investment Bank
ALBA	Alianza Bolivariana de los Pueblos de Nuestra América (Bolivarian Alliance for the People of our America)
APEC	Asia-Pacific Economic Cooperation
APEP	Americas Partnership for Economic Prosperity
ASCM	Agreements on Subsidies and Countervailing Measures
ASEAN	Association of Southeast Asian Nations
BIT	Bilateral investment treaty
BRI	Belt and Road Initiative
BRICS	Brazil, Russia, India, China and South Africa
BRIGC	BRI International Green Coalition
CBAM	Carbon Border Adjustment Mechanism
CELAC	Comunidad de Estados Latinoamericanos y Caribeños (Community of Latin American and Caribbean States)
CISCE	China International Supply Chain Expo
CO_2	Carbon dioxide
COP	Conference of Parties
CORFO	Corporación de Fomento de la Producción (Chilean Economic Development Agency)
DFC	US International Development Finance Corporation
DSM	Dispute Settlement Mechanism
ECI	Economic Complexity Index
ECLAC	Economic Commission on Latin America and the Caribbean
EU	European Union
EUDR	European Union Deforestation Regulation
EVs	Electric vehicles

FAO	Food and Agriculture Organization of the United Nationa
FDI	Foreign direct investment
FTA	Free trade agreement
G20	Group of Twenty
GATS	General Agreement on Trade in Services
GATT	General Agreement on Tariffs and Trade
GCECP	Global Clean Energy Cooperation Partnership
GDP	Gross domestic product
GHG	Greenhouse gas emissions
GNI	Gross national income
GVC	Global value chain
HVDC	High Voltage Direct Current
ICRSISC	International Cooperation on Resilient and Stable Industrial Supply Chains
ICSID	International Center for the Settlement of Investment Disputes
ICT	Information and communication technology
IGD	Inclusive green development
IIA	International investment agreement
IMF	International Monetary Fund
IPCC	Intergovernmental Panel on Climate Change
IPs	Industrial policies
IRA	Inflation Reduction Act
IRENA	International Renewable Energy Agency
ISDS	Investor-state dispute settlement
LAC	Latin America and the Caribbean
MAGA	Make America Great Again
MFN	Most favored nation
MNCs	Multinational corporations
NDB	National development bank
NDC	Nationally determined contributions
NGOs	Non-governmental organizations
OECD	Organization for Economic Co-operation and Development
OFDI	Outward foreign direct investment
OPEC	Organization of the Petroleum Exporting Countries
RELAC	Renewables in Latin America and the Caribbean
RR-LAC	The 11 resource-rich Latin American countries discussed in this book
S&DT	Special and differential treatment
SCO	Shanghai Cooperation Organization
SMEs	Small and medium-sized enterprises
TRIMs	Trade-related Investment Measures
TRIPS	Trade-related Intellectual Property Rights

UMSCA	United States, Mexico and Canada
UNCTAD	United Nations Commission of Trade and Development
UNDP	United Nations Development Programme
UNIDO	United Nations Industrial Development Organization
US	Unites States of America
WIPO	World Intellectual Property Organization
WTO	World Trade Organization

List of Tables

CHAPTER 1

Toward Inclusive Green Development in Latin America

Eva Paus and Rafael Domínguez

Abstract Latin American countries confront a triple challenge to development: growth-reducing structural change, limited social inclusion, and global warming. To address these challenges, we propose a development strategy with a green developmental state as the driver and broadly defined industrial policies at the core. We investigate the opportunities and challenges of inclusive green development (IGD) for 11 resource-rich Latin American countries. At the current juncture, two factors greatly facilitate the pursuit of such a strategy: (1) the global green transition which increases the demand for critical minerals and (2) the renewed legitimization of industrial policies in the Global North. In light of the urgency for action, limited financial resources, and the need for broad coalitions supporting IGD, governments have to leverage the interconnectivities among the three IGD goals to achieve double- and triple-win outcomes. While the space for action at the national level varies, an active and coordinated non-alignment strategy among Latin American governments would strengthen their ability to navigate the turbulent waters of strategic competition between great powers.

The original version of the chapter has been revised. A correction to this chapter can be found at https://doi.org/10.1007/978-3-032-08588-7_7

E. Paus, R. Domínguez, *Toward Inclusive Development in Latin America*, Palgrave Studies in Latin American Heterodox Economics, https://doi.org/10.1007/978-3-032-08588-7_1

Keywords Latin America • Growth-reducing structural change • Limited inclusion • Green transition • Heterodox economics • Inclusive green development • Industrial policies • Policy synergies • International political economy • Strategic non-alignment • Geo-economic and geopolitical context

We also resolve to create conditions for sustainable, inclusive, and sustained economic growth, shared prosperity and decent work for all, taking into account different levels of national development and capacities.
—UN 2030 Agenda for Sustainable Development (United Nations (2015))

Latin American countries confront a triple challenge to development: growth-reducing structural change, limited social inclusion, and global warming. Four decades of neoliberal policies have led to premature de-industrialization and a re-primarization of exports in South American economies, while producers in Central America and Mexico have become more integrated into the lower end of global value chains (GVCs) (Bértola & Ocampo, 2022; Torres & Ahumada, 2022). Economic and productivity growth has been low, with employment expanding more rapidly in relatively low-productivity sectors. Although poverty rates have declined significantly and there has been an expansion of public goods and improvements in human development (Ocampo & Titelman, 2023), structural heterogeneity and inequality of income and wealth continue at high levels, and large informal sectors demonstrate the limited creation of decent jobs (Jaimes & Matamoros, 2017; Palma, 2022).

Changing the nature of structural change and increasing social inclusion are demanding challenges in the current context, where the fourth industrial revolution, the rise of China, the Trump whirlwind, and a restructuring of geopolitical alliances are changing the global architecture of production and power. An equally urgent challenge is the need for a green transition, as rising global temperatures and increasingly severe weather patterns make fossil fuel-based growth unsustainable, everywhere including in Latin America.

A new development strategy is needed to address the triple challenge, with a green developmental state as the driver and broadly defined industrial policies at its core. The global green transition offers an opportunity for the resource-rich Latin American countries to address the triple challenge by leveraging their natural resources for more sustainable and green development, and thus overcome commodity dependence in the medium run. The green transition raises the demand for so-called critical minerals, many of which exist in abundance in Latin America. The influx of foreign exchange and the potential for appropriating a larger share of resource rents open the possibility for governments to embark on a new inclusive green development (IGD) strategy. There have been opportunities before, most recently the commodity super cycle of the 2000s, but countries did not take sufficient advantage of them. Will this time be different? That is the critical question we engage in this book. The answer, in good economics tradition, is 'it depends.'

In this book we focus on the contingencies shaping the adoption and implementation of IGD. Based on heterodox economics and international geopolitical economy considerations, we examine the conditions under which resource-rich Latin American countries may overcome the different challenges. We focus on 11 resource-rich Latin American countries, which together account for around 90 percent of Latin America's gross national income (GNI).[1] Throughout the book, we will use RR-LAC when we refer to the 11 resource-rich Latin American countries, and LAC when we refer to all of Latin America and the Caribbean.

We argue that a green developmental state is a sine qua non for the implementation of an IGD strategy, and broadly conceptualized industrial policies (IPs) are at the heart of such a strategy. The renewed recognition of the efficacy of IPs, especially in the Global North, makes it easier for Latin American governments to embrace and pursue them. In light of the urgency for action, limited financial resources, and the need for broad coalitions supporting IGD, governments have to leverage the interconnectivities among the three IGD goals to achieve double- and triple-win outcomes.

Even though the natural resource-rich economies of Latin America share key structural characteristics, we underscore the heterogeneity among countries in the region. As the gravity of the three major economic challenges (productivity-enhancing structural change, broader inclusion, greater contribution to a green transition) varies by country, so will policy

[1] The countries are Argentina, Bolivia, Brazil, Chile, Colombia, Ecuador, Mexico, Paraguay, Peru, Uruguay, and Venezuela. Excluding Venezuela for which there are no GNI data, they accounted for 83.6 percent of Latin America's GNI in 2023 (in current $ PPP) (World Development Indicators).

priorities. The possibilities for change are not the same either. They differ with state capacities, social capital, levels of inequality and informality, pragmatic leadership, and governments' willingness and ability to take actions to loosen the considerable external and internal constraints in policy and fiscal realms. Nonetheless, whatever the starting position, governments do not have a choice but to pursue IGD with broad IPs. Otherwise, the development challenges will continue to intensify.

The creation of coalitions in support of an IGD strategy may have to progress at different speeds, as the reduction of inequality may face greater opposition from elites than reducing emissions and increasing productivity. While the space for action at the national level varies, an active and coordinated non-alignment strategy among Latin American governments would strengthen their ability to navigate the turbulent waters of strategic competition between great powers.

In this introductory chapter, we present our theoretical framework, discuss the three major development challenges confronting Latin American economies, delineate the contours of an IGD strategy, and offer examples of policies for double- and triple-win outcomes. In the subsequent chapters, we discuss the economic and political challenges and opportunities for pursuing IGD in the current national and global contexts.

Theoretical Framework

Two questions drive our research: (1) How can the abundance in natural resources be transformed to support inclusive and green development? and (2) Will it be possible to take advantage of the global green transition to break away from extractivism by leveraging the very wealth of natural resources?[2] To answer these questions we use a theoretical framework, which integrates heterodox economics and international geopolitical economy. The framework combines the international political economy of structural change at the national level and its interrelations with international regimes. In both aspects, it underscores the importance of path dependency, power structures, and country- and time-specific context for

[2] Following Andreucci's (2023) definition of extractivism, we embrace two meanings of the term: (1) a mode of extraction of natural resources, characterized by large quantities of extracted material, little processing, and destined for exports, and (2) a mode of development where the redistribution of extractive rents is a central element in shaping the political economy of the country.

understanding the opportunities and challenges of implementing an IGD strategy. We follow the insights of the interdisciplinary and systemic approach of the dependency research program (Kvangraven, 2020; Palestini & Madariaga, 2021), which focuses on structures of production (technological capacities, organization of labor markets, structural heterogeneity) and particular constraints to peripheral development (technological and financial dependencies, unequal exchange).

On this basis, we posit that such a dependent development is possible, that there is room for a progressive agency, but that it faces considerable challenges due to internal and external structural constraints. It depends on the establishment of new political coalitions to sustain it and on international cooperation between like-minded Latin American countries and Northern partners in technological, financial, and trade issues (Porcile et al., 2023; Lema & Pérez, 2024; Villegas & Peña, 2024). A green developmental state is essential for the pursuit of renewed development.

The international geopolitical economy perspective highlights the centrality of the interactions between national and external actors, rules, and institutions in circumscribing the possibilities for implementing the new strategy, given historical and country-specific factors within a context of international rules and regulations and shaped by geo-economic spheres and the geopolitics of energy (Criekmans, 2023).

To explain the outcomes of development strategies and policies, it is necessary to consider political power relations within the state, the ideological orientation (the vision of development) of those who control it, institutional capacities to promote change, the government management of distributive conflicts that arise during the transition process, and the ability to navigate international regimes in order to secure sufficient policy space (Chang & Hope, 2021). In the Latin American context, this neo-developmentalist orientation toward the political economy of structural change and green transition is shared by the Economic Commission for Latin America and the Caribbean (ECLAC) school of thought, which has evolved from classical developmentalism (structuralism) to ecological new developmentalism (ecological neo-structuralism). The latter synthesizes post-Keynesianism with evolutionary economics giving rise to the three elements of ECLAC's recent political economy: Keynesian, Schumpeterian, and environmental efficiency.

The first element is the demand side of the Keynesian efficiency approach (structuralism), as a theory and strategy of development, which tried to overcome the balance of payments constraint and external vulnerability in explaining center-periphery external asymmetries, focusing on the need for state-led industrialization to transform the pattern of specialization, while also meeting the objectives of social inclusion and protection of the environment. The second element is the supply side of the Schumpeterian efficiency approach (neo-structuralism), which highlights the critical role of social and productive capabilities and industrial policies in fostering green catch-up from static to dynamic comparative advantages, within the context of slowing globalization (*slowbalization*) and energy transition as a core part of the fourth industrial revolution. And the third element is environmental efficiency (the ecological approach) which emphasizes the decoupling of economic growth from material use and carbon emissions following the Paris Agreement on Climate Change (Guarini & Porcile, 2016; Porcile, 2021; Porcile et al., 2023; ECLAC, 2024c).

This kind of ecological neo-structuralism is based on a big push investment toward sustainability (Sánchez et al., 2023; Porcile et al., 2023), seizing "the unique historical opportunity to leverage natural resource specialization for the development of new technologies and key sectors in the current and forthcoming technological revolutions" (Marín & Pérez, 2023, p. 52). The theoretical and policy proposal of ecological neo-structuralism connects with the new ecological developmentalism, which directly addresses ecological structural change through an eco-development national strategy, at the head of which is a new kind of developmental state (the environmental state) to promote green sectors and enable them to compete internationally through export-led industrialization reinforced by international cooperation (Guarini & Oreiro, 2022; Kastelli et al., 2023).

The global context of the green transition (geo-economic spheres and geopolitics of energy) also demands an approach from international geopolitical economy based on both cooperation and conflict in international relations. The role of power and politics underpinned by strong vested interests of incumbent agents (states, national oil companies, international oil and gas corporations, investment banks, global investment funds, renewable energy companies, transnational networks such as the International Renewable Energy Agency (IRENA), multilateral organizations such as the Organization of the Petroleum Exporting Countries and the International Energy Agency (IEA), environmental NGOs, and social movements) is key for understanding struggles about the green transition between elite factions (Agbaam et al., 2023; Kuzemko et al., 2024). As the production and, especially, refining and processing of *transition* metals are more concentrated than those of oil and natural gas, the geopolitical economy of the green transition is closely linked to power dynamics and highlights the existence of a "new international energy power structure and world energy order" (Yang et al., 2023, p. 684). The US, the EU, China, and Russia, are the main actors in the new geopolitical energy competition, while the developing country regions (and developing economies, whether they are winners or losers) as supporting actors are grouped into geo-economic spheres.

We believe that, with the right policies, it is possible to grow and 'green,' to decouple economic growth from fossil fuel use. We do not consider the concept of degrowth a viable approach for Latin American countries. Despite gaining prominence in academic sustainability debates, with explicit recognition since the 2022 IPCC report, the practical implementation of degrowth, grounded in strong sustainability, remains a significant challenge. Degrowth is an unsuitable strategy for Latin American economies, where growth, combined with redistribution, remains politically and socially justified as a means to improve living standards (Guarini & Oreiro, 2022).

Natural Resource Abundance and the Triple Challenge

Extractivism has dominated the economic dynamics and power structures in LAC for a long time. The composition of natural resource exports, the technology used to extract them, and the dominant actors have changed over the centuries; yet export dependence on primary products with low technological content has continued (see Table 1.1). Agricultural commodities dominate in Argentina, Brazil, Ecuador, Paraguay, and Uruguay; fossil fuels in Colombia and Venezuela; and mining in Bolivia, Chile, and Peru. Although commodities do not dominate Mexico's exports, we include the country here because it is large and resource-rich.

During the past two decades, natural resources have contributed to regional economic growth and helped address the social problems of poverty and, to a lesser extent, of inequality (Martins, 2023; Domínguez, 2023; Sánchez et al., 2023). Nevertheless, natural resource extraction cannot lead to sustainable inclusive development. The income elasticity of demand for exported commodities is lower than for imported manufactured goods, and commodity price booms lead to overvalued real exchange

Table 1.1 Commodity export dependence and reserves of critical minerals and fossil fuels

Countries	*Commodity export dependence (2019–2021)*				*Proven reserves (2020)*[a]			
	All commodities	*Agriculture*	*Energy*	*Mining*	*Critical minerals*	*Oil (a)*	*Gas (b)*	*Coal (c)*
Argentina	82.1	75.5	3.9	2.7	Lithium [2]	2.5	0.4	
Brazil	73.4	41.3	13.2	19.0	Lithium[16], graphite [2], nickel [4], rare earths [3]	11.9 [16]	0.3	6.6 [15]
Paraguay	81.9	79.3	1.9	0.7				
Uruguay	87.3	68.2	17.8	1.3				
Colombia	78.6	22.0	48.0	8.6		2	0.1	4.6 [16]
Ecuador	94.1	55.5	32.7	5.9		1.3		
Venezuela	73.5	3.8	68.1	1.7		303.8 [1]	6.3 [6]	0.7
Bolivia	94.6	18.9	27.1	48.6	Lithium [1]		0.2	
Chile	88.3	28.8	0.7	58.7	Copper [1], lithium [4]			
Peru	90.9	23.9	6.4	60.6	Copper [3], lithium [14]		0.7	0.3
Mexico	17.5	8.8	5.2	3.4	Copper [5], graphite [10], lithium [10]	6.1 [18]	0.2	1.2

Source: UNCTAD (n.d.), US Geological Survey (2023), Energy (2024)

[a]World ranking of the 20 largest suppliers in brackets, (a) billion barrels, (b) trillion cubic meters, (c) million tons

rates with negative consequences for national production, especially manufacturing. Extraction is not sustainable environmentally, as it has increased pressures on soil and water and sparked social-environmental conflicts with adjacent communities. Furthermore, the rise in global temperatures and projected weather catastrophes if temperatures rise more than 1.5–2°C above pre-industrial levels highlight the urgent need to move to clean energy sources (IPCC, 2023). As countries have embarked on a green transition, especially in parts of the Global North and China, the demand for fossil fuels is projected to peak within the next 10 years, though the second Trump Administration and some foot dragging in the EU may push the date back a bit.[3] At some point thereafter, fossil fuel exporters will be left with stranded assets.

In the short to medium run, however, resource extraction can be a critical facilitator of an IGD agenda. Countries can leverage natural resource wealth to reduce extraction and commodity export dependence in the future and develop alternative sources of production, employment, and tax revenue. The global green transition offers a window of opportunity, as Latin American countries possess more than a quarter of the world's major metal ore reserves considered critical materials: 47 percent of global reserves of lithium, 37 percent of copper, 24 percent of natural graphite, 17 percent of rare earths, 16 percent of nickel, and 14 percent of zinc (ECLAC, 2024a, p. 20). Table 1.1 provides details on the countries with significant reserves in critical minerals, including their ranking in global comparison. Continued extraction over the coming years can, however, not be a carte blanche for production as usual. Extraction can and needs to be made less destructive; the adoption of new technologies (e.g., direct lithium extraction) and the implementation of rules and regulations for best standards can reduce the environmental impacts and increase the benefits for surrounding communities (ECLAC, 2024a).[4]

Numerous studies have analyzed the development crisis in the region (Ocampo, 2004–2005; Paus, 2020; Pérez Caldentey & Vernengo, 2021; Martins, 2023; Ocampo & Titelman, 2023, Porcile et al., 2023; ECLAC, 2024b). Thus, we provide only a succinct summary of the three key challenges including 12 indicators in support. Although trends are generally similar across RR-LAC, there is also considerable heterogeneity. For each indicator, we distribute countries into three different groups: best performers, medium performers, and worst performers (see Table 1.2). For most indicators, the groups are based on a country's performance relative to the other RR-LAC. But even the best performers may not be doing well enough compared to the rest of the world or to what is needed for systemic transformation. Two indicators ('vulnerability to climate change' and 'economic complexity index') show RR-LAC's performance relative to all countries in the world included in the index.

[3] Estimates vary on the year when fossil fuel demand will peak. Demand has been declining in developed economies, but increasing in developing economies.

[4] The Initiative for Responsible Mining Assurance lists 400 requirements for social and environmental standards. But, to date, their audits of mines are only on a voluntary basis.

Table 1.2 The triple challenge: heterogeneity among RR-LAC

	Date(s)	ARG	BOL	BRA	CHI	COL	ECU	MEX	PAR	PER	URU	VEN
Emissions and energy use												
Change in CO intensity (CO2/$2011 PPP GDP)	2022/2002											
Change in GHG emission p.c.	2022/2002											
Change in energy intensity (MJ/$2017PPP GDP)	2021/2002											
Clean renewable energy/primary energy supply	2021											
Change in forest area	2020–1990											
Vulnerability to climate change												
Vulnerability to climate change ranking	2022											
Employment in agriculture/total employment	2022											no data
Export diversification & growth												
Economic Complexity Index ranking	2021											
Average annual productivity growth	1991–2021											
Gross fixed capital formation/GDP	2023–2013											no data

Social inclusion												
Palma ratio	2022											no data
Informal employment/total employment	2023								no data			no data

Range for groupings: best-performing group (green); medium-performing group (yellow); worst-performing group (red).

Change in CO intensity (CO2/$2011 PPP GDP)	(–16.5) –(–18.8)	(–9.6) –(–1.7)	13.7
Change in GHG emissions p.c. (%)	(–31) –(–21.8)	(–22) –(–10)	0–41
Change in energy intensity (%)	(–13.8) –(–22.3)	(–6.3)–(–4.7)	1.8–19.5
Clean renewable energy/primary energy supply (%)	50–55	14–21	< 10
Change in forest area (millions of ha) (%)	(–6.6) –(–9.4)	(–4.9)–(–2.1)	1.23 - 2.94
Vulnerability to climate change ranking (187 countries)	1–62	63–125	126–187
Employment in agriculture/total employment (%)	<10	11–17	25–32
Economic Complexity Index ranking (out of 133 countries)	1–40	42–82	83–133
Average annual productivity growth (%)	2–2.34	0.98–1.52	(–0.26) –0.59
Gross fixed capital formation/GDP (%)	22.2 –24.2	19 –21	16 – 17.7
Palma ratio (income share of top 1 % to bottom 40 %)	1.85 –2	2–2.7	3.5–4.6
Informal employment/total employment (%)	26.4–37	50.5–56.3	66.5–84.4

Sources: CO_2 intensity and GHG emissions: *Our World in Data*; energy intensity, employment share in agriculture, gross fixed capital formation ratio: World Development Indicators; share of clean renewable energy: CEPALSTAT; productivity growth: ECLAC (2024b); change in forested area: FAO (2024); informal employment share: ILO database; vulnerability to climate change: *Notre Dame GAIN*; economic complexity index: https://atlas.cid.harvard.edu/rankings; Palma ratio: ECLAC (2023a)

Lack of Productivity-Enhancing Structural Change

A fundamental development challenge in Latin America has been low productivity growth with productivity-reducing structural change. Productivity growth is a major driver of economic growth and a key source of international competitiveness. Compared to other developing country regions, Latin America and the Caribbean had the lowest productivity growth over the past 20 years.[5] A decomposition of productivity growth shows that nearly all productivity growth has come from growth within sectors, while the contribution from the across-sector component (which results from labor moving to sectors with different productivity) has been negligible and, in some countries, even negative (ECLAC, 2024b; Paus, 2020). An extreme case is Mexico, where labor productivity declined at an annual rate of 0.26 percent. Although within-sector labor productivity grew at 1.29 percent, the across-sector rate declined by 1.55 percent (ECLAC, 2024b, pp. 159–160); in other words, employment expanded significantly more in sectors with below average productivity levels.

Closely connected to low productivity growth is low innovation activity. In 2021, the innovation rate (expenditures on research and development as a share of gross domestic product, GDP) was only 0.54 percent for LAC. It was even lower in the RR-LAC, except for Brazil, whose innovation rate is twice the regional average (1.15 percent).[6] High export dependence on commodities together with low productivity growth translates into an export basket of low technological sophistication, as reflected in the rankings on the Economic Complexity Index (ECI) (see Table 1.1). Mexico's excellent ECI ranking (22nd in 2021) is deceiving. It does not reflect the state of domestic innovative and productive capabilities, but rather the exports from the maquila sector, which have low domestic value added (Caria et al., 2017). Indeed, in 2021, Mexico's innovation rate was only 0.27 percent.

The final factor capturing the economic situation is the low investment rate. Gross fixed capital formation as a share of gross domestic product (GDP) averaged 20 percent between 2013 and 2023 for the RR-LAC, ranging from a low of 16 percent in Argentina to a high of 24.2 percent in Chile. That is well below the 25 percent needed for sustained growth (Spence, 2012).

[5] In 2023, gross domestic product (GDP) per person employed was only 14.5 percent higher than in 2002. Over the same period, labor productivity had increased by 28.2 percent in Sub-Saharan Africa, 34.5 percent in the Middle East and North Africa, 126 percent in South Asia, and a whopping 280 percent in East Asia. World Bank. World Development Indicators. Online.

[6] https://agenda2030lac.org/estadisticas/banco-datos-regional-seguimiento-ods.html?indicator_id=3915&lang=es

Limited Social Inclusion

The second major development challenge in Latin America is limited social inclusion. Interpersonal inequality is a key characteristic of exclusion. The income share of the top 10 percent in LAC is still the highest among world regions (58 percent), and the ratio of the top one percent to the bottom 50 percent is the second highest globally (75.2).[7] Here, too, we find considerable differences across countries. Around 2021, the share of the population with an income below 50 percent of the median income varied from a low of 12 percent in Argentina to a high of 24.7 percent in Paraguay (ECLAC, 2022a). And the Palma ratio, which shows the ratio of the income of the top 10 percent to the bottom 40 percent, ranged from 4.6 in Colombia to 1.85 in Uruguay (ECLAC, 2023a). The distribution of wealth is extremely unequal, too. In 2022, the share of net wealth held by the top 10 percent was around 60 percent for most countries; for Brazil, Chile, and Mexico, it was around 80 percent.[8]

Inequality is not limited to income and wealth, of course. The vertical inequalities are accompanied by horizontal inequalities which reproduce social exclusion via job informality and unequal access to public services, based on attributes of age, gender, race, (dis)ability, residence, or migratory status (ECLAC, 2022b, 2023a, 2024b). The lack of job creation in the formal sector is particularly striking, but not surprising given the growth slowdown since the end of the commodity boom. Between 2013 and 2022, formal sector employment grew by only 3.3 percent in LAC (from 126.4 million to 130.4 million), while employment in the informal sector grew by 18 percent (from 101.2 million to 120 million). At 22.8 percent, employment growth in the informal sector was especially pronounced for women (ECLAC, 2024b, p. 176).

A large informal sector is a structural barrier to increased well-being, the ultimate goal of development, as informal sector workers tend to have lower incomes and no social benefits compared to formal sector workers. ECLAC (2023b) estimates that informal sector workers are four times more likely to live in low-income households. Irrespective of sector, firms in the informal economy tend to be small and have much lower productivity compared to large formal sector firms, a phenomenon captured by the concept of structural heterogeneity. Large informal sectors also mean a smaller tax base, and work against the development of a tax culture. Finally, lack of inclusion has major socio-political implications, as it promotes distrust in government and institutions.

[7] World Inequality Database (https://wid.world/data/)

[8] World Inequality Database (https://wid.world/data/)

The Unsustainability of Extraction and Fossil Fuel-Based Production and Consumption

The third challenge for Latin American development is the urgent need to reduce carbon emissions. Historically, developing country areas have been responsible for only a relatively small share of carbon emissions. Over the period 1850–2022, RR-LAC accounted for 9.9 percent of global greenhouse gas (GHG) emissions, compared to 18.2 percent for the US and 26.8 percent for the EU-27.[9] However, in 2022, their share in global GHG emissions was 8.6 percent, considerably higher than their share in global population (7.1 percent) and in GDP (6.6 percent).[10]

Over the past two decades, GHG emissions per capita, CO_2 intensity (emissions per $ of GDP), and energy intensity (energy used per $ of GDP) declined in most RR-LAC. CO_2 intensity was generally well below the world average (0.28 kg per international $ in 2022), but GHG emissions per capita were considerably above the global average in several countries (6.75 tons of CO_2 equivalent).[11] There are large differences not only across countries (see Chart 1.1), but also across income groups. In 2019, per capita annual emissions of the top 10 percent of income earners in LAC were 19.2 tons, compared to 4.7 tons for the middle 40 percent and two tons for the bottom 50 percent (Chancel et al., 2022, p. 121). Yet, environmental degradation tends to affect people in lower-income groups, where indigenous and Afro-descendant citizens and women are overrepresented, substantially more than those at the top, who can defend themselves better against climate change (Alcañiz & Gutiérrez, 2022).

Even though CO_2 intensity has declined, extraction has increased, in absolute and relative terms. Between 2002 and 2021, domestic extraction of materials per unit of GDP increased from 1.9 to 2.0 kg in the region.[12] Together with the relatively more inefficient use of materials (1.9 kg of material intensity vs. 1.3 kg worldwide)[13] and water ($12 of value added per cubic meter of water extracted vs. $19 worldwide), these figures reveal

[9] Authors' calculations based on ourworldindata.org. GHG emissions include carbon dioxide, methane and nitrous oxide, and land-use change.

[10] Population and GDP (in current international $) from World Development Indicators. The GDP data do not include Venezuela for which there are no data.

[11] GHG emissions per capita ranged from four tons in Peru to 12.5 tons in Uruguay.

[12] Material Flow Analysis Portal, https://www.materialflows.net/

[13] Material intensity is calculated as the ratio between domestic material consumption (in kilograms) and GDP (in constant 2010 dollars), with domestic material consumption being the sum of domestic extraction and material imports minus material exports (Global Material Flows Database).

the huge environmental cost of maintaining and increasing primary-export specialization.

Emissions and energy use intensity have to decline considerably more in LAC, like in the rest of the world, if countries are to reach the goals they specified in the nationally determined contributions (NDCs) under the Paris Agreement.[14] Some RR-LAC have advanced considerably more than others in the move to renewable energy. In 2021, clean renewable energy made up more than half of the primary energy supply in Uruguay and Paraguay, while it accounted for less than 10 percent in Argentina, Bolivia, Chile, and Mexico. If we include non-clean renewables (firewood, cane sugar, and derivatives), the share of renewables increases to 100 percent in Paraguay, and nearly 50 percent in Brazil. Hydro is the most important source of clean energy in many countries. A downside of heavy reliance on hydro is that it leads to greater volatility in energy supply, as climate change has increased the occurrences and duration of droughts.

Without more aggressive action on climate change mitigation and adaptation, countries will face large costs in output, income, employment, and fixed assets, as global warming will bring more extreme and frequent weather events. ECLAC (2024b, p. 202) estimates that, in the absence of mitigating actions, climate change will lead to a reduction of 0.6 percentage points in annual growth between 2025 and 2050 in LAC, with 42.7 million fewer jobs.[15] Countries with a high share of output and employment in agriculture and tourism are particularly vulnerable to the impacts of climate change. They include Bolivia and Ecuador, which globally rank in the bottom third of Notre Dame's GAIN Index, a broad measure of a country's vulnerability to climate change (World Wildlife Fund, 2024, pp. 26–27).[16]

A green transition is not only about decarbonization, but also about halting and reversing loss in biodiversity and forest coverage. Biodiversity

[14] Under the Paris Agreement, countries submit a new NDC every five years, with successively increasing commitments. For details on individual country NDCs see https://unfccc.int/NDCREG. Among the RR-LAC, Argentina, Brazil, Chile, Colombia, Peru, and Uruguay have announced commitments to reach carbon neutrality by 2050, while Argentina, Chile, Colombia, Mexico, and Uruguay have published long-term strategies of low carbon development toward 2050 (De Miguel et al., 2024, p. 18)

[15] For the global level, Strinati et al. (2024) estimate the cost of keeping temperature increases below 1.5 C by 2050 at $266 trillion. But the loss in a 'business as usual' scenario until the end of the century is projected to be five times higher: $1266 trillion.

[16] The Vulnerability Index looks at six life-supporting areas: food, water, health, ecosystem service, human habitat, and infrastructure (https://gain-new.crc.nd.edu/ranking/vulnerability)

is critical for the supply of ecosystem services which are vital for the security of food, air, and water, and play a critical role in neutralizing a sizeable share of CO_2 emissions. The Amazon is one of the world's largest carbon sinks, and Brazil, Colombia, Ecuador, Mexico, Peru, and Venezuela are among the 17 megadiverse countries in the world.[17]

Compared to other world regions, the forested area in South America has shrunk the most, 130 million hectares between 1990 and 2020.[18] This is often due to large agricultural exports based on soy and cattle ranching.[19] Cattle ranching constitutes a double blow for the climate due to the combination of deforestation and methane release. In 2022, agriculture accounted for an average of 34.7 percent of GHG emissions in RR-LAC, compared to 12.1 percent globally (see Table 1.3).

Biodiversity in the region has significantly decreased as well. Between 1970 and 2020, the Living Planet Index for Latin America declined by 95 percent, compared to 76 percent for Africa, 60 percent for Asia and the Pacific, and 35 percent for Europe and Central Asia.[20]

Table 1.2 illustrates the heterogeneous performance of the RR-LAC with respect to the three major economic challenges. Overall, Chile has the relatively best performance (eight times in the best-performing group) followed by Brazil, Mexico, and Uruguay. Bolivia and Ecuador, on the other hand, have the relatively worst performance (six and five times, respectively, in the worst-performing group). Nonetheless, relative performance varies by indicator. For example, Chile, Mexico, and Uruguay are in the 'worst-performing' group with respect to the increase in CO_2 emissions, while Bolivia is in the 'best-performing group' regarding a decline in CO_2 emissions and inequality. The heterogeneity gives some indication of where different countries might concentrate their policy efforts. However, being in the best-performing group in an intra-regional context does not always translate into adequate performance in an internationally comparative context, e.g., with respect to productivity growth.

[17] World Economic Forum (2024). A country is considered megadiverse if it has at least 5000 plants that naturally occur within its borders including the marine ecosystem.

[18] It shrank by 106 million hectares in Africa, stayed roughly the same in North America and Central America, and actually increased in Asia and Europe (FAO, 2024)

[19] Commodity production (soy and pasture for beef production) accounts for two-thirds of deforestation in Latin America (ECLAC, 2024a).

[20] The Living Planet Index (https://www.livingplanetindex.org/) is based on trends of population of vertebrate species from marine, freshwater, and terrestrial habitats.

Table 1.3 Greenhouse gas emissions by sector, 2022 (in %)

	Agriculture	*Buildings*	*Fuel exploitation*	*Industrial combustion*	*Power industry*	*Processes*	*Transport*	*Waste*
Argentina	37.0	10.6	10.8	4.8	11.9	6.9	13.3	4.7
Bolivia	45.1	5.2	13.9	3.7	6.0	2.9	19.1	4.2
Brazil	45.7	3.7	5.4	6.5	3.9	5.0	16.4	13.5
Chile	9.1	6.8	2.8	11.9	24.0	10.4	22.2	12.7
Colombia	34.0	5.3	8.9	6.0	7.0	6.9	18.0	13.9
Ecuador	19.2	10.4	17.1	4.6	7.5	4.6	27.5	9.0
Mexico	15.0	4.5	10.7	7.1	15.8	18.5	17.9	10.5
Paraguay	68.8	1.6	2.5	0.7	0.0	3.2	19.5	3.7
Peru	20.8	6.2	10.0	8.4	12.1	5.7	25.0	11.8
Uruguay	64.0	3.1	1.3	2.8	1.7	1.7	10.8	14.7
Venezuela	22.6	1.8	28.9	6.6	5.7	7.9	18.6	7.9
Simple Average	*34.7*	*5.4*	*10.2*	*5.7*	*8.7*	*6.7*	*18.9*	*9.7*
Global	12.1	7.1	11.6	12.2	27.5	9.4	15.1	5.1

Source: Authors' calculations based on European Commission. EDGAR database online, https://edgar.jrc.ec.europa.eu/

The Need for Systemic Change: Bringing a Green State In

A continuation of extraction cum market-led strategies cannot lead to inclusive green development. To address the triple challenge of greater social inclusion, more productivity-enhancing structural change, and better environmental sustainability requires the adoption of a new development strategy, a strategy which aims at systemic change.

Government leadership and actions are indispensable for the implementation of the new strategy, with green industrial policies and full attention to inclusion. The current global context has heightened the importance of bringing the state back in, this time as a green developmental state. Over the past decades, China's economic rise and the rapid unfolding of the fourth industrial revolution have dramatically increased competitive pressures. They have moved the goal posts for middle-income countries, making the ability to compete internationally on the basis of productivity rather than low wages more important than ever. In addition, countries face a situation of compressed development (Whittaker et al., 2010), which demands government action in support of both high- and low-productivity producers.

In this context, governments, in consultation with and supported by a broad coalition of stakeholders, must establish and implement a strategic vision for economy-wide changes. A vision which prioritizes activities that have the greatest potential for successful outcomes given country-specific economic structure, resources, and policy space. The implementation of a green government-led strategy is a marathon, not a sprint. Step-wise actions and processes, with adjustments along the way, will move countries closer to the goal over time.

Government regulations and incentives have to make it attractive for the private sector to invest in sustainability and activities with higher value added. At different levels of government, institutional capacities are needed for the co-development of the requisite technological, institutional, and financial capabilities and support for the private sector in the development of productive capabilities (Cimoli et al., 2017; Kastelli et al., 2023). Appropriate macroeconomic policies have to complement green industrial policies. Governments may have to create markets for new green sectors or products, e.g., through procurement of green technology; and they play a pivotal role in advancing social and environmental justice, which includes offering alternatives for those who lose out when extraction declines. They have to bring together key stakeholders in ongoing consultations on the effectiveness of policies. Public investment is required for the co-development of green and digital infrastructure; and governments play a critical in procuring more financial resources, through tax reforms, development banks, and access to international funding sources.

There are many instances where government policies will address primarily one of the three goals, or an aspect of it. However, given the urgency for action on all three fronts, the limitations of resources and capabilities, and the need to establish broad-based coalitions in support of the new strategy, we argue that it is vital for governments to maximize the use of policies which leverage the interconnectivities among the goals to achieve win-win or even win-win-win outcomes (see Fig. 1.1). We offer a few policy examples below.

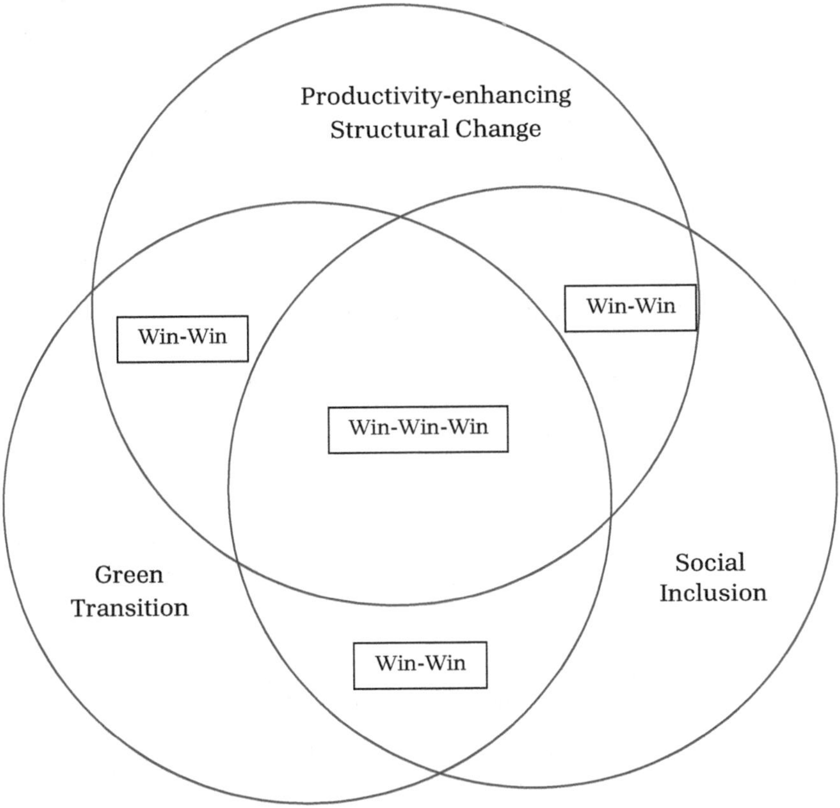

Fig. 1.1 Leveraging synergies for inclusive green development

Examples of Policies With Win-Win-Win Outcomes

The literature on the green transition distinguishes between activities which clean existing 'brown' industries and those which are completely new and may be at the heart of a new 'green' sector (Arup and Oxford Economics, 2023).[21] In both areas, policies can lead to a triple win.

A top priority in cleaning 'brown industries' has to be more efficient energy use in existing production, e.g., building insulation, more fuel-efficient cars, a reduction in energy waste in production, and electricity generation and distribution of energy (Pollin, 2020). The transport sector and the power industry are two obvious targets for green investments in Latin America (see Table 1.2). Research shows that clean energy investments lead to significant job creation compared to continuing with a fossil fuel infrastructure. Estimates range from an increase of 75 percent in Brazil to 350 percent in Indonesia (Pollin, 2021). More broadly, Saget et al. (2020) estimate that a 35 percent reduction of GHG emissions in LAC by 2030 leads to a net job increase of 15 million.

The development of new green technologies, products, and services may also result in a triple win. Since green technologies tend to be sector-specific with few spillovers to other sectors, their development differs with respect to the knowledge needed and engineering principles involved (Lema & Pérez, 2024). That may be an advantage or a disadvantage for LAC. The advantage is that domestic producers do not have to compete with long-established producers, but can develop a new green technology from the get-go, potentially leapfrogging and contributing to catch-up. The disadvantage is that domestic producers may not have the requisite resources in knowledge and other areas to develop and market a new technology. Producers in countries with large domestic markets and a diversified manufacturing sector may be in a better position to advance in new green areas, e.g., Argentina, Brazil, and Mexico. Nonetheless, there are possibilities for green technology advancement in niche areas for producers in all countries, as shown by the growth of new environmental services in Uruguay and Chile (see Chap. 2).

[21] In these categories, Arup and Oxford Economics (2023, pp. 22–24) list dozens of green activities, with hundreds of sub-activities. They include green infrastructure projects, reforestation and rehabilitation, sustainable agriculture processes, green building construction, production of electricity from renewables, manufacture of low carbon products, green fuel, waste remanufacturing and refurbishing, recycling and related activities, public transport greening activities, water treatment, sewage services, green finance, environmental education, and support for environmental professional services.

While green energy investments increase inclusion through greater employment, their impact on inequality is not unequivocal. If employment expansion is concentrated in higher-skilled workers, inequality will increase, as they command a higher wage. But if green activities lead to greater employment of less skilled workers (e.g., construction of new infrastructure or refitting of houses), then they will reduce inequality.

Making production in agriculture more sustainable (e.g., regenerative farming and greening of food production) also generates a triple win by improving the quality of soil and water, reducing GHG emissions, improving productivity (as 'green' products and production processes command a higher price in the markets of the Global North), and increasing inclusion, if it raises the income of small and medium-sized producers.

Targeted support for small and medium-sized enterprises (SMEs) in different sectors can be a win on all three fronts. People without access to banking services cannot receive remittances or transfers in case of climate shocks; and people without Internet have limited access to information, be it meteorological information to inform planting decisions, information about input prices and technologies, or information about new markets.[22] Thus, coupling policies to expand financial inclusion with reaching 100 percent electricity and broadband coverage will give producers greater ability to improve productivity and expand market access and green production.

Examples of Policies With Win-Win Outcomes

Investments in information and communication technology (ICT) can also advance the green transition and structural transformation if governments steer it in the right direction. They can reduce the environmental impact of the ICT sector itself and enhance innovations in the green economy sector (Lema & Pérez, 2024; Fearn, 2024).

A number of studies have shown that inequality contributes to poorer environmental outcomes (Knight et al., 2017; Apeti et al., 2025; Hou et al., 2024). Political economy factors play an important role in explaining this finding. A high concentration of wealth and income translates into

[22] In 2021, 122 million people in Latin America did not have a bank account (Mejía & Saaverdra, 2022). ECLAC (2022), https://www.cepal.org/en/insights/basic-water-and-electricity-services-key-sectors-transformative-recovery-latin-america-and#:~:text=Currently%20in%20Latin%20America%20and,the%20context%20of%20the%20war

concentration of political voice at the high end which lowers the introduction of environmental legislation (Apeti et al., 2025). Low-income households, on the other hand, have little political voice to oppose environment-degrading activities from which they benefit little, but whose costs they bear to a disproportionate extent (Boyce, 2023, 2024).

Thus, addressing inequality directly with the right policies can leverage the synergies between social inclusion and a green transition. Governments can steer investment in environmental protection to lower-income communities. In the agricultural sector, policies can internalize positive externalities and compensate people for providing environmental services, e.g., compensate small farmers for maintaining crop diversity (Boyce, 2024). That would reduce rural poverty and safeguard agricultural biodiversity. Important measures to reduce or stop deforestation and increase inclusion involve regularizing land tenure, recognizing and protecting the rights of indigenous communities, promoting sustainable production, and government regulations and enforcement (De Miguel et al., 2024).

Carbon taxes and caps can be designed with explicit consideration of their distributional consequences. A specific carbon tax is progressive if levied on transport fuel, but regressive if imposed on heating. Similarly, a generalized carbon tax by itself tends to be regressive, since the higher prices for fossil fuels have a larger impact on the budget of lower-income households. But the negative distributional impact can be counteracted through targeted transfers to these households (Pollin, 2020). In a survey of 40,000 people from 20 countries, Dechezleprêtre et al. (2025) find that support for a carbon tax increases when it is progressive, e.g., when carbon taxes are combined with cash transfers to low-income households.

Boyce (2024) makes the case for universal carbon dividends, based on the argument that natural resources belong equally to all people. He proposes that the revenue from a carbon tax or the permit auctions in case of a carbon cap should be rebated in equal dividends to every resident in a country. An equal dividend will be progressive, as it constitutes a larger income share of poorer households; and such action may also make a green transition politically more palatable.[23]

[23] In Colombia, one of the few Latin American countries with a carbon tax, distributional considerations have played a role in the assignation of the revenue generated. It first went to the Fund for Sustainable Environment and Rural Sustainable Development and subsequently to the Peace Fund of Colombia, with 70 percent earmarked for post-conflict solutions (Giovanni et al., n.d.).

Not Always Win-Win

One of the areas where a win-win is more doubtful and will likely require separate actions is the impact of the fourth industrial revolution on the creation of decent employment. The rise of China and the fourth industrial revolution have increased the urgency for middle-income countries to compete internationally on the basis of productivity growth rather than lower wages. Thus, if government policies incentivize and support productivity growth, producers of traded goods can become internationally competitive and potentially generate more employment.

Incorporating elements of the fourth industrial revolution more broadly, e.g., automation through robotics, ICT, and artificial intelligence (AI), will likely increase firm productivity. But what about the impact on employment and distribution? The literature on the impact of new technology on employment in developing economies is limited, and the evidence is ambiguous. In a study of 22 sectors in 10 developing countries (including Brazil), Plumwongrot and Pholphirul (2023) analyzed firm responses regarding innovation and employment intention in 2019. They found that when a firm considered investing in new technology it reduced the probability of employment by 0.9 percent. Studying the risk of automation jobs in 11 developing countries, Egana del Sol (2020) found that the percentage of jobs that are highly automatable varied between 7.7 and 42.2 percent. In Bolivia, the only Latin American country in the study, the percentage was 27.5 percent. Of course, in the context of economies with large informal sectors, the percentage of jobs that can be automated is relatively small to start with. Nonetheless, it speaks to the challenge of creating decent jobs on a sufficiently large scale.

On the other hand, Maloney and Molina (2019) do not find much evidence of labor-displacing automation in developing countries. Indeed, the number of machine operators and assemblers actually increased in developing countries, possibly as a result of MNCs relocating to developing countries in order to combine the use of robots with lower-cost labor. Nonetheless, they find incipient polarization in Mexico and Brazil, the two RR-LAC with the largest manufacturing sectors, a possible effect we noted already.

While we do not know the future impact of the new technological revolution on social inclusion in Latin America, the evidence to date does not suggest a straightforward translation from productivity growth to inclusion. In light of the discussion above, it is quite likely that productivity-enhancing structural change will not generate enough decent jobs. Thus, measures to increase well-being in other ways become even more important. That includes making tax structures more progressive, advancing toward universal social services, expanding social protection, and supporting wage increases in non-traded sectors like the care sector. Concomitantly, investments in education, health, and skills will have a positive impact on social inclusion. In the medium term, they may also advance the green transition and production in higher value added and green activities, as people acquire the requisite skills.

Organization of the Book

The global green transition offers a historic opportunity for RR-LAC to address the key challenges they face: growth-reducing structural change, limited inclusion, and global warming. In the introductory chapter, we laid out the contours of an IGD strategy for systemic change. In the following chapters, we will analyze key opportunities and challenges for the implementation of such a strategy. We situate the analysis in the current economic and political contexts, with an emphasis on the interactions between national and international structures and power constellations. We suggest possible actions to leverage the opportunities and address the challenges.

Chapter 2 focuses on IPs, which have to be at the heart of an IGD strategy. Combining structural economics, green IPs, and a mission-based approach, Paus analyzes the conditions for successful IP outcomes, investigates different possibilities for upgrading and diversification in RR-LAC, and explores the opportunities and limitations of significant foreign-owned production, especially from China. She argues that government leadership and sufficiently broad-based agreement on IPs are the foremost conditions for IP success. In their absence, other factors cannot compensate. But when they exist, the other factors become critical: capabilities, continuity, transparency, win-win policies, and a persuasive narrative.

In Chap. 3, Paus analyzes two key factors which circumscribe the space governments have for implementing an IGD strategy: the commitments and demands stemming from international trade and investment arrangements, and the financial resources available to achieve the desired goals. She proposes possible actions to broaden the space, both at the international and the national level. Internationally, the rules need to be made compatible with the Sustainable Development Goals (SDGs), and thus with the implementation of an inclusive green transition; and financial resources for a green transition have to grow considerably. Nationally, governments can increase fiscal space in numerous ways, importantly—in the current context—by appropriating a larger share of the natural resource rent. And governments can expand their policy space by terminating international investment agreements, which include an investor-state dispute settlement mechanism.

In Chap. 4, Domínguez discusses the conditions necessary to build development-oriented coalitions that promote an IGD transition to break away from extractivism by leveraging the very wealth of natural resources. This strategy impacts state–society relations, requiring an analysis of values, interests, and historical context, across the dividing lines of vertical and horizontal inequalities. He argues that despite structural constraints there is potential for progressive agency behind dependent development. Factors such as social stratification, rising expectations, demographic structure, and strong concern about inequalities suggest potential electoral support for IGD. However, challenges arise due to political dynamics, changing social preferences, and internal polarization. Domínguez argues that transformative political leadership supported by development-oriented coalitions is crucial for overcoming the middle-income trap and achieving an inclusive green transition.

In Chap. 5, Domínguez examines the external geopolitical and geo-economic context influencing an IGD strategy, highlighting the increased volatility and uncertainty with the second Trump presidency. He connects structural dependency theory with world-systems analysis to explain Latin America's weaker international power position. Nonetheless, he argues that national governments retain agency to pursue dependent development, using the geopolitical landscape as an opportunity for inclusive green transformation. He uses the concept of "development by invitation" to explore the context of possible partnerships with the US, the EU, and China. He concludes that progressive governments in Latin America can navigate these challenges through strategic non-alignment, leveraging agreements with major powers to drive an IGD transition in the face of global strategic competition.

In Chap. 6, we conclude with a summary of the elements conditioning the success of an IGD. Based on the analysis in Chaps. 2, 3, 4, and 5, we highlight some of the strength factors for each of the RR-LAC to embark on an IGD strategy.

References

Agbaam, C. et al. (2023). *The political economy of sustainable energy transitions: A literature review and a research agenda* (IZE Working Papers Series, 23/3).

Alcañiz, I., & Gutiérrez, R. A. (2022). *The distributive politics of environmental protection in Latin America and the Caribbean*. Cambridge University Press. https://doi.org/10.1017/9781009263429

Andreucci. (2023). Extractivism. In B. M. Haddad & B. D. Solomon (Eds.), *Dictionary of ecological economics terms for the new millennium* (pp. 222–223). Edward Elgar.

Apeti, A. E., et al. (2025). Wealth inequality and carbon inequality. *Ecological Economics, 227.*, pN.PAG-N.PAG. 1p. https://doi.org/10.1016/j.ecolecon.2024.108406

ARUP & Oxford Economics. (2023). *The global green economy. Capturing the opportunity.* https://www.arup.com/insights/the-global-green-economy-capturing-the-opportunity/

Bértola, L., & Ocampo, J. A. (2022). La economía latinoamericana durante las primeras décadas del siglo XXI. *El Trimestre Económico, 89*(1), 353, 39–71. https://doi.org/10.20430/ete.v89i353.1425

Boyce, J. (2023). Environmental consequences of inequality. In E. Padilla & J. Ramos-Martín. Encyclopedia of ecological economics (200–204). Edward Elgar.

Boyce, J. (2024) *Inequality and the environment* (Working Paper 603). Political Economy Research Institute University of Massachusetts.

Caria, M., Carrera, M., & Domínguez, R. (2017). Can the monkeys leave the export processing zones? Exploring the maquiladora bias in the economic complexity index in Latin America. *Journal of Economics and Development Studies, 5*(1), 20–28. https://doi.org/10.15640/jeds.v5n1a3

Chancel, L et al. (2022). *World inequality report 2022*, wir2022.wid.world.

Chang, H. J., & Hope, C. (2021). The political economy of structural change. In L. Alcorta, et al. (Eds.), *New perspectives on structural change: Causes, and consequences of structural change in the global economy* (pp. 676–696). Oxford University Press.

Cimoli, M., et al. (Eds.). (2017). *Políticas industriales y tecnológicas en América Latina*. CEPAL.

Criekmans, D. (2023). Geopolitics, geoeconomics, and energy security in an age of transition towards renewables. In D. Sholten (Ed.), *Handbook on the geopolitics of the energy transition* (pp. 20–43). Edward Elgar.

De Miguel, C., et al. (2024) *Necesidades de financiamiento y objetivos climáticos en América Latina y el Caribe*. CEPAL, Documentos de Proyectos (LC/TS. 2024.47)

Dechezleprêtre, A., et al. (2025). Fighting climate change: International attitudes toward climate policies. *American Economic Review., 115*(4), 1258–1300. https://doi.org/10.1257/aer.20230501

Domínguez, R. (2023). Miradas estructurales sobre los extractivismos. In H.J. Burchardt, C. Gárgano & L. Christel (comps.), ¿De la sustentabilidad al desarrollo? Entre el extractivismo verde y la transformación socioambiental (pp. 155–176). CLACSO.

ECLAC. (2022a). *Social panorama of Latin America and the Caribbean 2022: Transforming education as a basis for sustainable development.* Economic Commission for Latin America and the Caribbean.

ECLAC. (2022b). *Towards transformation of the development model in Latin America and the Caribbean: Production, inclusion and sustainability.* Economic Commission for Latin America and the Caribbean.

ECLAC. (2023a). *Social panorama of Latin America and the Caribbean. Labour inclusion as a key axis of inclusive social development.* Economic Commission for Latin America and the Caribbean.

ECLAC. (2023b). *Fiscal panorama of Latin American and the Caribbean, 2023.* Economic Commission for Latin America and the Caribbean.

ECLAC. (2024a). *Natural resources outlook in Latin America and the Caribbean, 2023.* Economic Commission for Latin America and the Caribbean.

ECLAC. (2024b). *Economic survey of Latin America and the Caribbean 2024: Low growth trap, climate change, and employment trends.* Economic Commission for Latin America and the Caribbean.

ECLAC. (2024c). *Fiscal panorama of Latin America and the Caribbean 2024. Fiscal policy for addressing the challenges of climate change.* Economic Commission for Latin America and the Caribbean. (LC/PUB.2024/5-P).

Egana del Sol, P. (2020). *The future of work in developing economies: What can we learn from the South?* (GLO Discussion Paper No. 883). Global Labor Organization (GLO), Essen.

European Commission. *Emissions database for global hemispheric research (EDGAR).* https://edgar.jrc.ec.europa.eu/

FAO. (2024). *Global forest resources assessment 2020.* https://www.fao.org/interactive/forest-resources-assessment/2020/en/

Fearn, N. (2024, March 26). AI is accelerating the energy transition, Say industry leaders. *Financial Times.*

Giovanni, E., Khalid, F., & Richards, K. (n.d.). *Carbon tax in Colombia.* Gnarly Tree Sustainability Institute. https://gnarlytreesustainability.com/wp-content/uploads/2022/07/Case-5_Colombia.pdf

Guarini, G., & Oreiro, J. L. (2022). An ecological view of new developmentalism: A proposal of integration. *Brazilian Journal of Political Economy, 42*(1), 244–255. https://doi.org/10.1590/0101-31572022-3310

Guarini, G., & Porcile, J. (2016). Sustainability in a post-Keynesian growth model for an open economy. *Ecological Economics, 126*, 14–22. https://doi.org/10.1016/j.ecolecon.2016.03.0050921-8009

Hou, A., Liu, A., & Chai, L. (2024). Does reducing income inequality promote the decoupling of economic growth from carbon footprint? *World Development, 173*. https://doi.org/10.1016/j.worlddev.2023.106423

IPCC. (Intergovernmental Panel on Climate Change). (2023). *Climate change 2023*. Synthesis report. IPCC.

Jaimes, P., & Matamoros, G. (2017). ¿Qué sucedió con el *casillero vacio* del desarrollo de América Latina 30 años después? *Problemas del Desarrollo, 48*(191), 9–26. https://doi.org/10.1016/j.rpd.2017.11.002

Kastelli, I., Mamica, L., & Lee, K. (2023). New perspectives and issues in industrial policy for sustainable development: From developmental and entrepreneurial to environmental state. *Review of Evolutionary Political Economy, 4*(1), 1–25.

Knight, K. W., Schor, J. B., & Jorgensen, A. K. (2017). Wealth inequality and carbon emissions in high-income countries. *Social Currents, 4*, 403–412. https://doi.org/10.1177/2329496517704872

Kuzemko, C., et al. (2024). Rethinking energy geopolitics: Towards a geopolitical economy of global energy transformation. *Geopolitics, 29*(5), 1807–1830. https://doi.org/10.1080/14650045.2024.2351075

Kvangraven, I. H. (2020). Beyond the stereotype: Restating the relevance of the dependency research programme. *Development and Change, 52*(1), 76–112. https://doi.org/10.1111/dech.12593

Lema, R. & Pérez, C. (2024). *The green transformation as a new direction for techno-economic development* (UNU-MERIT Working Papers Series, 2024-001).

Maloney, W. F., & Molina, C. (2019). *Is automation labor displacing in the developing countries, too? Robots, polarization, and jobs*. © World Bank. http://hdl.handle.net/10986/33301 License: CC BY 3.0 IGO

Marín, A., & Pérez, C. (2023). Nuevas perspectivas para el desarrollo en base a recursos naturales: una visión neo-schumpeteriana para América Latina. In J. Sánchez & M. León (Eds.), *Recursos Naturales y Desarrollo Sostenible: Propuestas teóricas en el contexto de América Latina y el Caribe* (pp. 33–55). CEPAL.

Martins, H. (2023). Development versus structural heterogeneity: Trajectories of economic growth and income inequalities in Latin American countries from the 1980s. *International Journal of Political Economy, 52*(2), 213–233. https://doi.org/10.1080/08911916.2023.2241801

Mejía, D., & Saaverdra, M.. (2022*) Financial inclusion in Latin America: How far have we come?* CAF (Development Bank of Latin America and the Caribbean). https://www.caf.com/en/knowledge/views/2022/12/financial-inclusion-in-latin-america-how-far-we-have-come/#:~:text=Although%20the%20proportion%20of%20people,lower%2C%20of%200.7%20percentage%20points

Ocampo, J. A. (2004–2005) Beyond the Washington Consensus: What do we mean? *Journal of Post Keynesian Economics 27* (2), 293–314.

Ocampo, J. A., & Titelman, D. (2023). Rethinking development in Latin America. *Journal of Human Development and Capabilities, 24*(4), 569–591. https://doi.org/10.1080/19452829.2023.2264005

Palestini, S., & Madariaga, A. (2021). Introduction: Dependency as a research program: From situations to mechanisms of dependency. In A. Madariaga & S. Palestini (Eds.), *Dependent capitalisms in contemporary Latin America and Europe* (pp. 1–25). Palgrave Macmillan. https://doi.org/10.1007/978-3-030-71315-7_1

Palma, J.G. (2022). Latinoamérica es la región con el menor crecimiento de la productividad en el mundo desde las reformas neoliberales. La nueva trampa del ingreso medio: rentas fáciles no generan precisamente élites schumpeterianas. *El Trimestre Económico, 89*(3), 355, 943–977. https://doi.org/10.20430/ete.v89i355.1595.

Paus, E. (2020). Innovation strategies matter: Latin America's middle income trap meets China and globalisation. *The Journal of Development Studies, 56*(4). https://doi.org/10.1080/00220388.2019.1595600

Pérez Caldentey, E., & Vernengo, M. (2021). Financialization, premature deindustrialization, and instability in Latin America. *Review of Keynesian Economics, 9*(4), 492–511. https://doi.org/10.4337/roke.2021.04.03

Plumwongrot, P., & Pholphirul, P. (2023). Are robots stealing jobs? Empirical evidence for 10 developing countries. *Economics of Innovation and New Technology, 32*(6), 873–889. https://doi.org/10.1080/10438599.2022.2051020

Pollin, R. (2020). The industrial policy requirements for a global climate stabilization project. *International Review of Applied Economics, 35*(3–4), 389–406. https://doi.org/10.1080/02692171.2020.1755239

Pollin, R. (2021). Defending the global commons through a Global Green New Deal. *Social Research, 88*, 75–98.

Porcile, G. (2021). Latin American structuralism and neo-structuralism. In N. Foster-McGregor et al. (Eds.), *New perspectives on structural change: Causes, and consequences of structural change in the global economy* (pp. 50–71). Oxford University Press. https://doi.org/10.1093/oso/978019850113.003.0003

Porcile, G., et al. (2023). New directions in Latin American Structuralism: A three-gap model of sustainable development. *European Journal of Economics and Economic Policies: Intervention, 20*(2), 266–281. https://doi.org/10.4337/ejeep.2023.0105

Saget, C, Vogt-Schilb, A. & Luu, T. (2020). *Jobs in a net-zero emissions future in Latin America and the Caribbean.* Inter-American Development Bank and International Labour Organization.

Sánchez, J., León, M., & Porcile, G. (2023). Hacia un neoestructuralismo ecológico. In J. Sánchez & M. León (Eds.), *Recursos Naturales y Desarrollo Sostenible: Propuestas teóricas en el contexto de América Latina y el Caribe* (pp. 13–31). CEPAL.

Spence, M. (2012). *The next convergence: The future of economic growth in a multispeed world*. Macmillan Publishers.

Strinati, C., Alberti, C., Melling, B., & Baudry, C. (2024). Top-down climate finance needs. *Climate policy initiative*. https://www.climatepolicyinitiative.org/publication/top-down-climate-finance-needs/

Torres, S., & Ahumada, J. M. (2022). Las relaciones centro-periferia en el siglo XXI. *El Trimestre Económico, 89*(1–353), 151–195. https://doi.org/10.20430/ete.v89i353.1432

U.S. Geological Survey (2023). *Mineral commodity summaries 2023*. https://doi.org/10.3133/mcs2023

UNCTAD. (n.d.). *The state of commodity dependence*. https://unctad.org/topic/commodities/state-of-commodity-dependence

United Nations. (2015). *Transforming our world: The 2030 agenda for sustainable development*. Sustainabledevelopment.un.org

Villegas, B., & Peña, A. M. (2024). Development, democracy, and dependence in the Southern Cone: political coalitions, stabilizing mechanisms, and their hazards. *Review of International Political Economy, 32*(1), 29–52. https://doi.org/10.1080/09692290.2024.2380869

Whittaker, D., et al. (2010). Compressed development. *Studies in Comparative International Development, 45*(4), 439–467. https://doi.org/10.1007/s12116-010-9074-8

World Economic Forum. (2024). *World environment day: An A-Z of the world's 17 megadiverse countries*. https://www.weforum.org/agenda/2024/06/environment-day-biodiversity-world-megadiverse-countries/

World Wildlife Fund. (2024). *2024 Living Planet report – A system in peril*. World Wildlife Fund.

Yang, Y., Xia, S., & Quian, X. (2023). Geopolitics of the energy transition. *Journal of Geographical Sciences, 33*(4), 683–704. https://doi.org/10.1007/s11442-023-2101-2

CHAPTER 2

Industrial Policies for Inclusive Green Development: Challenges and Opportunities for Resource-Rich Latin American Countries

Eva Paus

Abstract Industrial policies (IPs), broadly understood, are essential for the implementation of an inclusive green development strategy. I argue that a combination of structural economics, green IPS, and a mission-based approach is the most appropriate approach to the conceptualization and implementation of IPs. I analyze the conditions for successful IP outcomes, investigate the possibilities for upgrading and diversification in research-rich Latin American countries, and explore the opportunities and limitations of significant foreign-owned production, especially from China. Government leadership and sufficiently broad-based agreement on IPs are the foremost conditions for IP success. In their absence, other factors cannot compensate. But when they exist, the other factors become critical: capabilities, continuity, transparency, accountability, coordination, win-win polices, and a persuasive narrative.

Keywords Green developmental state • Industrial policies • Conditions for policy success • Upgrading and diversification • Direct foreign investment • China • Government leadership • Critical minerals • Systemic change • Productive capabilities

E. Paus, R. Domínguez, *Toward Inclusive Development in Latin America*, Palgrave Studies in Latin American Heterodox Economics, https://doi.org/10.1007/978-3-032-08588-7_2

Rome wasn't built in a day, but they were laying bricks every hour.
—John Heywood (1546)

An inclusive green development strategy in Latin America aims for systemic change toward productivity-enhancing structural change, greater inclusion, and a reduction in greenhouse gas emissions. Industrial policies (IPs) are a sine qua non for the implementation of such a strategy. Historically, IPs referred to intentional government actions to change the size and structure of production toward higher value added activities in manufacturing. Today, the concept comprises a broader scope of intentional government policies, both with respect to the goals they may address (e.g., employment creation, productivity increase, decarbonization) and the sectors where such goals may be achieved (e.g., different types of services, different activities in agriculture, in addition to manufacturing). In other words, today's industrial policies are more versatile and transversal.

A number of Latin American governments leveraged the commodity super cycle of the 2000s to reduce poverty, but there were no systematic attempts to diversify the economy. To the extent IPs have been used at all, they have not been systemic, but often marginal; there is not enough cooperation among key actors; there is little vision and medium- and longer-term planning, and scant accountability and continuity across administrations (Castillo & Ominami, 2024; ECLAC, 2024a). The demonstrated success of IPs in some Asian countries—especially China (Kemp & Never, 2017) and the Asian Tigers—speaks to their effectiveness, as do sectoral pockets of excellence in Latin America (e.g., the aeronautical sector in Brazil, the pharmaceutical sector in Brazil and Costa Rica, the wine industry in Chile, and IT services in Argentina, Chile, and Uruguay) The challenge is to move from pockets of excellence to a broad and systemic approach.

In this chapter, I analyze the factors conditioning the success of IPs, and their use for productivity-enhancing structural change in natural resource-rich LAC countries (RR-LAC). I also explore the opportunities and limitations stemming from significant foreign-owned production, especially from China, given its prominence in the region. Government leadership and sufficiently broad-based agreement on IPs are the foremost conditions for IP success. In their absence, other factors cannot compensate. But when they exist, the other factors become critical: capabilities, continuity, transparency, win-win polices, and a persuasive narrative.

Industrial Policies on Center Stage

While neoclassical economics allows for IPs to correct market failures (negative externalities that drive a wedge between social costs and market prices, coordination failures, and information failures), structural economics considers IPs essential for changing the structure of the economy. Since demand elasticities and productivity of products and activities differ, it matters what you produce and export (Hausmann et al., 2007). Indeed, structural change drives economic growth and transformation (Ocampo, 2017). Whether, in that process, a country should conform to static comparative advantage or defy it is the subject of ongoing debate (Lin & Chang, 2009).

What is not under debate, however, is that the acquisition of productive capabilities takes time and needs to be supported by IPs. Since first articulated by Alexander Hamilton and Friedrich List in the eighteenth and nineteenth centuries, the infant industry argument has provided an important rationale for industrial policy. Latecomers in the development process will not develop dynamic comparative advantages and catch up without IPs (Cimoli et al., 2009). That was true historically for today's industrialized countries as well as for latecomers that advanced considerably after WWII. IPs are critical for the development of new productive capabilities in a sustained and dynamic manner and for the build-up of a national innovation system, especially in middle-income countries (Amsden, 2001; Fagerberg & Srholec, 2008).

In recent years, the understanding of IPs and their rationale has expanded in two important ways. The first is the incorporation of climate goals. With growing awareness of the need to cap the increase in global temperatures, it has become increasingly important and urgent to integrate decarbonization into IPs with the broader objective of social well-being and structural transformation (Tagliapietra & Veugelers, 2021; Anzolin & Lebdioui, 2021). Through regulation and polices focused on changing the demand and supply side of energy use, green IPs are critical for steering consumers and producers away from a fossil fuel-based economy.

The mission-driven approach to development is the second extension of the scope of IPs (Mazzucato, 2013). It emphasizes the importance of governments taking the lead in identifying goals and shaping markets, and sharing in the profits of companies which were able to develop and thrive because of government support. It asks for a fundamental rethinking of the role of the state, where the goals of IP are not sector specific, but policies focus on development and the common social and environmental good, transversally and systemically (Mazzucato & Monaco, 2024).

I suggest that the most appropriate approach to the conceptualization and implementation of IPs for inclusive green development combines elements of structural economics, green IPs, and a mission-based approach. The structural approach emphasizes the importance of shifting production to higher value added activities; green IPs stress the need for infusing industrial policies with an eye toward addressing climate change; and the mission-driven approach focuses on the need for systemic change and comprehensive and cohesive policies beyond sectoral policies.

A key difference between the context of the 2000s and the 2020s is the broader acceptance of industrial policies for development, in the dominant economic paradigm as well as in political practice. During the 2000s, the Washington Consensus still reigned supreme, albeit often in a modified version with greater attention to the role of institutions (Gallagher, 2016). Nonetheless, even when governments in the Global North preached the virtue of small government and market efficiency for the allocation of resources—roughly from the 1980s onwards—IPs continued to be an important part of their own policymaking (Block, 2008; Mazzucato, 2013). To wit, the projects that have come out of the Defense Advanced Research Projects Agency in the US and the development of Airbus in Europe.

Over the course of the last decade, however, IPs have moved from the sidelines to center stage, in the academy and in policymaking around the world. It is no longer only heterodox economists who advocated for IPs even when the market-led strategies of the Washington Consensus dominated policy recommendations (Amsden, 2001; Chang, 2003; Cimoli et al., 2009; Ocampo et al., 2009; Stiglitz & Lin, 2013; Wade, 2018; Oqubay et al., 2020). These days, a broader set of economists (Juhász et al., 2023b) and prominent international organizations including the IMF explicitly highlight the importance for economic development of the "policies that shall not be named," as two IMF economists famously called them (Cherif & Hasanov, 2019). In the policy realm, it is not only governments in the Global South that are pursuing IPs, but also—and above all—in the Global North, from the EU to Japan to the US. It is the extensive and explicit use of IPs in the Global North which has re-established their legitimacy globally, providing broad opportunities for Latin American governments to follow suit.

Using a text-based approach, Juhász et al. (2023a) find that the use of industrial polices has more than doubled since 2009, in absolute and relative terms. Evenett et al. (2024) identify 2580 industrial policies for 2023 alone: 98 plans and strategies, 1031 firm-specific interventions, and 1451 policies and regulations.[1] Advanced economies accounted for 70.9 percent of IPs, with China, the EU, and the US responsible for nearly half (47.7 percent).

The Paris Agreement with countries' commitments under the Nationally Determined Contributions (NDCs) has been one driving force behind the rise of green IPs (Juhász & Lane, 2024). Prominent examples include the Green New Deal in the EU (2019) and the Inflation Reduction Act (IRA) in the US (2022). The growing geo-economic and political competition between the US and China and the disruption of global supply chains during COVID-19 are additional reasons for the increasing adoption of IPs in the Global North. As countries found themselves with limited domestic production of critical medical supplies and industrial inputs for many sectors of the economy, the pandemic laid bare the dangers of hyper-globalization of supply chains.

Taiwan Semiconductor Manufacturing Company (TMSC), a stellar example of successful industrial policies, is today the largest global chip manufacturer producing around 90 percent of the world's super-advanced semiconductor chips (Hamrin, 2024).[2] In response to supply chain disruptions and the vulnerability of Taiwan in the context of growing tensions between the US and China, the US and the EU have adopted a slew of IPs to increase chip production in their own countries, e.g., the US CHIPS Act (2022) and the EU Chips Act (2023).

In addition to policies to localize semiconductor production, governments in the Global North have launched various initiatives to achieve or maintain international competitiveness in advanced and frontier technology. Examples are Japan's New Economic Policy Package (2017) aimed at the application of AI and big data in industries; the EU's Industrial Policy

[1] The IPs include import and export barriers, domestic and export subsidies, localization policies, public procurement policies, and trade finance.

[2] TMSC received significant funding from Taiwan's national development fund and the country's sovereign wealth fund.

Strategy (2019); France 2030 with 10 sectoral goals and $40 billion over five years; Germany's National Industrial Strategy (2019); and the Advanced Research Projects-Energy (ARPA-E) (2009) and Advanced Research Projects-Health (ARPA-H) (2022) in the US (DiPippo et al., 2022).

A new rationale for IPs has been the US emphasis on national security. Jake Sullivan, National Security Adviser under the Biden Administration, refers to the combination of economic aims and national security concerns as the New Washington Consensus. In a 2023 speech at the Brookings Institution, he argued:

> A modern American industrial strategy identifies specific sectors that are foundational to economic growth, strategic from a national security perspective, and where private industry on its own isn't poised to make the investments needed to secure national ambitions….This is about crowding in private investment.

The second Trump Administration has intensified the use of the national security argument. This time, however, in an incoherent and perverted way, with indiscriminate tariff imposition, but no strategic industrial policy.

In the Global South, China is the most prominent example of successful IPs. Consecutive five-year plans laid out priority goals which were supported with a barrage of transversal and specific policies. The 'Made in China 2025' plan (2015) aimed to increase domestic content in core industries; and the 14th Five-Year Plan (2021–2025) focuses on self-sufficiency in core technologies (DiPippo et al., 2022). As a result of successive IP packages, willingness to change policies when they did not work, required technology transfer from multinationals investing in China, relatively low wages, and a favorable exchange rate, China now dominates global production and exports in many industries. China is an example of what IPs can achieve when the government pursues a mission-oriented approach.

In recent years, we have seen growing resource nationalism in developing economies, as they have become frustrated with the poor results of Washington Consensus policies. To capture higher value added segments in natural resource-based value chains, a number of governments have required or incentivized further processing of natural resources before they are exported.

The question is not whether Latin American governments should adopt IPs or not. IPs have to be center stage for countries to have a decent shot at inclusive green development. Rather, the question is how they can do it and which conditions increase the likelihood for success. That is the focus of the rest of this chapter.

Conditions for Success

The success of industrial policies depends on a complex set of conditioning factors. Their existence or the possibilities to create them depend, in turn, on country-specific characteristics including path dependency, government capacity, political power constellations, and relations among parties and between the government and different economic and social groups. Chapter 3 focuses on the fiscal and policy space needed for IPs for inclusive green development, and Chap. 4 on the possibilities of establishing political coalitions in support of an inclusive green agenda or part of it.

Continuing Government Leadership and Buy-In From Key Constituencies

A sine qua non for IP success is a government that clearly articulates the key objectives of the development strategy, the specific goals that IPs are supposed to achieve in the short, medium, and long run, and the steps to achieve them. There has to be flexibility in execution, and learning from mistakes in the process, and a willingness to abandon initiatives and companies, when things do not work out. Governments have to "cross the river by feeling the stones."

Government leadership is also needed to address the distributional implications of IPs. IPs, especially but not only green IPs, normally generate winners and losers. When some activities become uncompetitive as a result of IPs or the phaseout of fossil fuels, there will be losers, and policies have to include compensating actions. Extractive industries tend to be regionally concentrated, so that a reduction in extractivism needs to be accompanied by job-generating alternatives in the respective locations. That will also make the 'destructive' elements of IPs more acceptable.

In the green transition in China and South Korea, both countries sequenced policies such that 'creative' elements preceded 'destructive' ones (Thurbon et al., 2023). Policymakers viewed the creation of a clean energy industry strategically as a necessary prerequisite for fossil fuel phaseout. They provided support and incentives for fossil fuel producers to redirect investments to emerging industries, and for automakers to produce electric vehicles (EVs).[3] More generally, with appropriate government support, capabilities in the extraction of gas and oil might be repurposed toward the integration of a clean energy supply chain (Lebdioui, 2024, p. 58). It may be possible to transform state-owned oil companies into state-owned energy companies, following the example of the Danish Oil and Natural Gas Company (ECLAC, 2024b, p. 229).

Time inconsistencies between the incurrence of the costs of IPs and the realization of their benefits can pose a serious challenge to their public acceptance. Constituencies generally do not consider a longer-term time horizon when it comes to the results of government policies. That tends to be forgotten sometimes when theorizing about IPs. For example, New Developmentalism highlights the importance of getting macro policies right, especially a real exchange rate that is not overvalued and an interest rate that incentivizes private sector investment. However, the politics of time inconsistencies question the practical feasibility of some theory-based proposals.[4]

In an analysis of US voter behavior related to natural disasters, Healy and Malhotra (2009) find that voters reward an incumbent presidential party for having delivered disaster relief, but not for preventative spending to avoid the disaster in the first place. They conclude (p. 402) that "voters are unwilling to spend on natural disasters before the disasters have occurred." Others argue that external threats (e.g., foreign aggression or the threat thereof) enable governments to rally support for government policies, e.g., in South Korea (Studwell, 2013). Thurbon et al. (2023) suggest that the factors motivating China and Korea to embark on a green

[3] Thurbon et al. (2023, p. 48) highlight in the Korean case "the state's targeted support for established automaker Hyundai in its efforts to pioneer local and global fuel cell electric vehicle markets and for coal-invested KEPCO to lead the nation's charge into green hydrogen for baseload power and other purposes."

[4] Oreiro (2024), for example, advocates a real devaluation and an export tax on soybeans and beef in Brazil. Although the devaluation will lead to a decline in real income, he suggests that workers will accept it because, in the medium run, salaries will arise again as there will be more production in higher-productivity areas. Similarly, soy and beef producers are predicted to accept the export tax, as the resulting decline in production will lead to increased prices (given Brazil's global importance in these two markets) and thus will not affect their profits in the medium run.

transition were changing geopolitics, especially for China, and growing environmental problems, especially air pollution.

Bottom-up pressure can also lead and support governments to adopt specific IPs. The demands may come in response to a disaster (e.g., public demands to shut down nuclear power plants in Germany after the Fukushima meltdown in 2011) or from social movements that enabled progressive governments to come to power in the first place. Chapter 4 analyzes in greater detail the importance of social movements in supporting a progressive agenda.

Regardless of whether there is an acute emergency or not, IPs need to be designed strategically to garner acceptance. Policies might focus on creation before destruction, or creation along with destruction, on rechanneling investments by existing corporations into new activities, or on a multi-pronged approach that includes employment creation and other elements. Juhász and Lane (2024, p. 38) suggest that a "wide range of objectives may make it more feasible to pass [such] legislation by appealing to multiple constituencies." Bergquist et al. (2020) find there is greater support for climate policies in the US if they are combined with policies like minimum wage increases or affordable housing. Based on survey results of 40,000 respondents from 20 countries, including Brazil and Mexico, Dechezleprêtre et al. (2025) show that support for climate policies is greater when they are progressive, e.g., when clean energy infrastructure is funded with progressive taxes or carbon taxes are combined with cash transfers for lower-income households.

Crafting a powerful positive narrative which explains the benefits of the policies is critical for establishing and maintaining political support. Thurbon et al. (2023, p. 53) argue that the governments of South Korea and China used developmental environmentalism as a political legitimization strategy. In Korea, they focused on 'green growth' and, in China on 'ecological civilization.' Mazzucato (2024), too, highlights the power of narrative. For example, an administration could make the case for a 'progressive green growth' narrative, with climate finance as an investment in the country's future, not a cost, and as the generator of additional investments and employment creation in related sectors. Dechezleprêtre et al. (2025) find that people's support for public climate-focused policies increased considerably after they were shown a video of how climate policies worked, e.g., their impact on emissions and distribution.

Since the goals of IPs are generally not achieved during the tenure of one administration, basic agreement on key goals across administrations is critical for the success of IPs. Unfortunately, such continuity is often lacking, in Latin America and elsewhere. For example, in 2001, the Lagos Administration in Chile (2000–2006) initiated the High Technology Investment Promotion and Attraction Program which offered one-time subsidies for employing higher-skilled workers ($25,000/worker) and unskilled workers ($5000/worker), with the proviso that companies stay in Chile for at least 10 years. The Piñera government (2010–2014) abolished funding in 2010, after the program had generated $2 billion in service exports (Agosin, 2023, p. 127). Similarly, attempts to establish the Fund for Innovation and Competitiveness under Bachelet (2006–2010) were watered down by business and discarded by Piñera (Bril-Mascarenhas & Madariaga, 2019). In Peru, the National Plan for Productive Diversification under the Humala Administration (2011–2016), with the establishment of public–private partnerships in key areas, was discarded by the following Kuczynski government (2016–2018).

Importantly, there are also examples of IP continuity across administrations, with different parties in power. Costa Rica (starting in the 1980s) and Ireland (starting in the 1970s) pursued and expanded IPs to attract foreign direct investment (FDI) with generous incentives. Over time, they shifted the mix of inward FDI from labor-intensive products (e.g., clothing) to IT, pharmaceuticals, and digital services (Paus, 2005). Uruguay's wind energy revolution over the past 15 years is another example. It demonstrates how the confluence of key factors conditioning IP success led to an impressive outcome: green IPs in response to an economic emergency, a multi-party agreement across different party administrations, a powerful narrative, and a policy package assuring private sector profitability for an extended period (see Box 2.1).

Which Industrial Policies?

IPs have to align with country-specific goals. Which IPs are most appropriate depends on the goal, and the political, fiscal, and international policy space. Even within those parameters, policies need to be responsive to changes in circumstances.

Over the years, scholars have proposed different taxonomies for IPs (Cimoli et al., 2009; Andreoni, 2017; Weiss & Seric, 2020; Agosin, 2023). With respect to green IPs, Lebdioui (2024, p. 30) makes the useful distinction between demand-side policies and supply-side policies. Demand-side policies include public procurement, fiscal incentives for low-carbon

Box 2.1: The Wind Energy Revolution in Uruguay

Uruguay has become world-renowned for its wind energy revolution. In one decade, the country went from a situation with basically no wind energy installations to wind power accounting for 30 percent of installed electric power in 2020. Government vision, leadership, and implementation were critical.

Spark for the action: When the Uruguayan economy was doing well in the late 2000s, the growing demand for energy led to a huge increase in the import bill and blackouts. Uruguay has no fossil fuels domestically, and had already used rivers for hydropower. Internationally, oil prices were rising, and there was an oversupply of capital goods linked to wind energy generation.

Government leadership: Ramón Méndez Gaitan, a physicist by training, had developed a plan for a just transition to renewable energy, with a focus on wind energy (lots of wind turbines on empty land) and management of energy from intermittent sources (wind, biomass, hydro). In 2008, President Tabaré Vasquez from the Frente Amplio (2005–2010) invited Gaitan to become the head of the National Energy Agency and implement the plan. The next government, José Mujica from the Movement of Popular Participation (2010–2015), continued the strategy after getting acceptance from all political parties. Thus, a long-term plan was in place with the backing of the whole political system.

Role of government and private sector: A vertically integrated government agency, Usinas y Transmisiones Eléctricas del Estado (UTE), established in 1977, has the monopoly in power distribution. Following auctions, UTE signed power purchase agreement contracts with private producers, which guaranteed an energy price for 20 years. This ensured demand as well as profitability for private investors, most of whom were foreign companies. In addition, there were tax incentives.

Inclusion: UTE pays rent to the owners of the land where the turbines operate. To date, 50,000 jobs have been generated, roughly 3 percent of the labor force.

Linkages: There are few linkages in the capital goods sector given limited technological capabilities and the speed of the transition. But there has been considerable capability development in services linked to renewable energy generation, and some companies are now exporting their services (e.g., Ventus, SEG Engineering, CCI).

Narrative: Wind is the best option because it is cheaper and does not depend on oil price fluctuations. Energy prices will be lower and more predictable than under oil.

Path dependency: In spite of Washington Consensus policies, there was continuity, legitimacy, and strength of public institutions, as well as organizational capabilities across institutions. In addition, there was a large public university with considerable research activity. Academics worked for years to develop software specifically designed to handle energy dispatch to manage intermittent energy sources.

Potential challenge: Energy providers are paid in US dollars, but consumers pay with Uruguayan pesos.

Sources: Benites Lazaro and Serrani (2023), Meadows (2023), Méndez Galain (2023), Ponce (2024).

technology consumption, local content requirements, import constraints, price controls, and environmental regulation. And supply-side policies cover fiscal incentives for low-carbon technology production, subsidized credit, public investment in related infrastructure, public financing for R&D support, green skills development, and public provision of a clean energy matrix to firms.

While subsidies are more easily accepted than price increases, developing economies generally have limited fiscal space for financial incentives. In high-income countries, financial grants account for over 40 percent of green IPs, followed by state loans and trade finance. In middle-income countries, on the other hand, state loans dominate followed by price stabilization. And local content requirements tend to be more prominent in middle-income countries, with the US IRA a significant exception (Juhász & Lane, 2024).[5] Estimates for spending on productive policies in 2021

[5] For example, as of January 13, 2025, the US government had announced $32.2 billion in grants under the CHIPS Act (https://www.semiconductors.org/chips-incentives-awards/)

are 0.67 percent of GDP in Argentina, 0.33 percent Chile, and a mere 0.08 percent in Mexico (BID, 2024). Brazil spent 0.33 percent in 2019. These numbers pale in comparison with the 1.48 percent for China (2019) (DiPippo et al., 2022).[6] With limited fiscal space, IPs other than financial incentives become all the more important, especially regulation and government creation of demand.[7]

One of the lessons from the import-substitution period in Latin America (and elsewhere) is the importance of conditioning government support on measurable deliverables, thus simulating the 'carrots and sticks' of the market mechanism. South Korea, for example, conditioned government support on firms exporting a growing of share of output. If conditionalities are not enforced or absent, as often occurred in LAC, there is no pressure on firms to reach the expected goals. Conditionality creates a deal between the public and private sector and can make benefits contingent upon the achievement of public goals, e.g., employment generation or use of clean technology (Mazzucato & Rodrik, 2024).

Another important factor for IP success is government capabilities, broadly defined.[8] Governments have to conceive IPs in a comprehensive way, as a set of mutually reinforcing measures needed to achieve a specific goal. For example, when a government offers tax incentives for the purchase of energy-efficient vehicles, but there is insufficient investment to widen the network of battery charging stations—as happened during the Correa Administration in Ecuador (Anzolin & Lebdioui, 2021)—then success will be limited. Furthermore, governments have to be able to coordinate across ministries and institutions so that policies are aligned

[6] Not included in DiPippo's data are agriculture and energy subsidies, infrastructure and education, regional development programs, SME programs, and non-quantifiable measures (e.g., public procurement).

For the period 2015–2019, Hufbauer and Jung (2021, p. 15) calculate the total cost of US IPs at $2.225 billion at the federal level (2.4 percent of the federal budget) and $2.454 billion at the state level (1 percent of state-level budgets).

[7] The US Advanced Research Projects Agency-Energy (ARPA-E), established in 2007, provides research support for new technology to extract, process, and store minerals to address societal, economic, and environmental issues. But the biggest challenge is whether the demand will be there. Will companies and people be willing to pay a premium for technologies that are greener and more socially friendly?

[8] Yülek et al. (2020) find that the difference in success of the automobile industry in South Korea and Turkey is not that one adopted industrial policies and the other did not. Rather, they both adopted industrial policies, but Turkey had weaker state capacity which was reflected in the quality of industrial policies.

and mutually reinforcing, e.g., between the Ministries of the Economy, the Environment, Education, and Finance.

National development banks (NDBs) play a critical role in advancing an IGD agenda. They can support structural transformation and inclusion by directing funds to specific sectors and firm sizes, provide funding in local currency and for long-term projects that the private sector can or will not finance, secure international funding at better rates, lend counter-cyclically, foster public–private partnerships, and share risks with private sector investors (Griffith-Jones & Ocampo, 2018). NDBs, like IPs, can condition their loans on specific outcomes. However, for NDBs to be impactful, they have to work in the context of a clearly articulated development strategy, be transparent, and have sufficient scale.

The legacy of past development strategies is a key difference between most Latin American countries and the Asian countries where IPs have often been used more successfully. A long tradition of a developmental state nurturing local manufacturing capacity and export competitiveness and of collaborative government–business relations has facilitated the green transition drive in China and South Korea (Thurbon et al., 2023). In Latin America, in contrast, several decades of neoliberal policies have led to premature de-industrialization and a decline in the public sector's institutional capacity. Castillo and Ominami (2024, p. 211) refer to widespread "institutional precarity," notwithstanding examples of outstanding institutions for structural transformation.[9] Path dependency is not fate, though. But to broaden the space it frames in Latin America, it is all the more important that efforts become strategic and forceful.

Upgrading and Diversification

Latin American governments have to use IPs strategically to leverage the opportunities offered by the global green transition, opportunities to reduce their dependence on natural resources in the medium run, upgrade production, diversify their economies, and start to develop dynamic comparative advantages. In general, there are three—not mutually

[9] For SMEs and entrepreneurship: SEBRAE (Brazil), SERCOTEC, INDAP (Chile), INNPULSA (Colombia); for science and technology: INTI and INTA (Argentina), EMBRAPI (Brazil), ANID (Chile), CONACYT (Mexico), ANII (Uruguay); for enterprise development: CORFO (Chile), ANDE (Uruguay); for development banks: BRCA, BNA, and BICE (Argentina), BNDES and BNB (Brazil), COLDEX (Colombia), NAFIN (Mexico); and for attraction of foreign direct investment: InvestChile, Uruguay XXI.

exclusive—possibilities for new comparative advantages: localization of higher-value segments in critical minerals, development of renewable energy sources, and use of the additional revenue to develop higher value added activities in other sectors. To the extent that Latin American countries have pursued any of these options to date, the focus has been on the first two. However, more strategic and comprehensive policies are needed to take advantage of the window of opportunity that the green transition offers.

Moving Up the Value Chain in Critical Minerals

A number of observers have highlighted the development potential of critical minerals for Latin American countries (IEA, 2023; ECLAC, 2023). Argentina, Brazil, Bolivia, Chile, Mexico, and Peru have significant proven reserves of critical minerals (see Table 1.1). Lithium is of particular interest, as it is key for lithium-ion batteries, which are the heart of electric vehicles (EVs) and for which demand is highest among critical minerals (ECLAC, 2024b). Bolivia ranks #1, Argentina #2, and Chile #4 in proven lithium reserves in the world. To date, most governments have not taken a strategic approach to the localization of a critical minerals value chain.

In a growing number of countries in the Global South, the demand for critical minerals has given rise to resource nationalism. Indonesia, for example, issued a ban on the export of raw nickel in 2014, relaxed it in 2017, and reinstated it in 2020. The Democratic Republic of the Congo (2023) restricted the exports of raw ores; Namibia (2022) and Zimbabwe (2023) banned exports of raw lithium; and Ghana (2024) prohibited exports of raw bauxite, lithium, and iron ore (Reilly, 2024). In each case, the motivation was to foster domestic production beyond extraction.

Governments resorted to export restrictions, performance requirements, local content requirements, and market reserve policies. In the past, developing countries used a lot of tariff measures; now there many more measures taxing or restricting exports. Around 30 percent of critical mineral exports (by value) had some export restrictions in 2022, compared to only 5 percent in 2019 (Javorcik et al., 2023). But between 2009 and 2022, the restrictions on critical mineral exports increased substantially less in Latin America than in other areas: 11 percent compared to 22 percent in Southeast Asia and 54 percent in Africa (BID, 2024).

Even though most Latin American countries with lithium reserves have declared lithium a mineral of strategic interest, none has banned the export of lithium or other critical minerals to force greater domestic value production at home. Indeed, governments have demonstrated very different interests in upgrading in the lithium value chain. Bolivia adopted the most state-centric approach, with the National Strategy for the Industrialization of Evaporite Resources in 2010 under Morales (2006–2019). Extraction, processing, and industrialization were to remain in the hands of the state, while the private sector could participate in the commercialization. But the strategy did not come to fruition due to poor hydro-geological conditions, regional disputes over the distribution of rents, and lack of the requisite know-how, funding, and infrastructure (Johnson et al., 2024; Milanez & Dorn, 2024). In late 2024, Bolivia signed an agreement with China's CBC to invest $1 billion in lithium plants in the country.

Chile's approach to the governance of domestic development of the lithium value chain dates back to 1979, when exclusive ownership of lithium was given to the state. In 2023, after several intermittent steps, the Boric Administration (2022–2026) rolled out a National Lithium Strategy. It included the establishment of a national lithium company and a public–private partnership with the state as the major shareholder (ECLAC, 2023). CORFO, the Chilean Development Organization, renegotiated contracts with Albermarle (US) and SQM (mainly Chilean), which require them to contribute to R&D and sell up to 25 percent of their production at a reduced price to companies which add value to lithium in Chile (Becker Toro, 2024).

Countries with a large domestic market and prior manufacturing capabilities may be better able to move toward greater industrialization in lithium (Lebdioui, 2024). But that presupposes a well-defined national plan and coherent support policies, which Brazil does not have. In Brazil, the National Mining Plan 2050 adopted in 2022 did not include any concrete plan for lithium (Milanez & Dorn, 2024).

In Argentina, provinces have control over natural resources, and they have not established any requirements for foreign firms to contribute to local development (González Jáuregui, 2024). And in Mexico, the López Obrador Administration (2018–2024) passed a Mining Law Reform in 2022, which gave *Litio para México* control of all new lithium exploration and exploitation contracts (Milanez & Dorn, 2024, p. 7).

Even when governments do not intend to move up the lithium value chain, they can and should capture a higher share of the resource rent through royalties and taxes. There is considerable space for government action, not only with respect to lithium, but also regarding mineral extraction more broadly. At one extreme is Brazil where all minerals which are exported as raw materials are exempt from state and federal taxes, and royalties are set at a mere two percent of gross revenue. Royalties are 3 percent of net revenue in Argentina, 3 percent of export value in Bolivia, and 7.5 percent in Mexico. The only exception is Chile, where royalty rates are applied on a marginal basis linked to price, growing from 6.8 percent to 40 percent (Milanez & Dorn, 2024, p. 8). In 2022, Chile's fiscal revenues from lithium were $5 billion or 6.4 percent of total fiscal revenues (Becker Toro, 2024). That's huge, especially since fiscal space is tight, as we discuss in the next chapter.

Of course, there are challenges to developing downstream processing. They include the high level of financing, the complexity of technological know-how, access to other critical minerals (cobalt, graphite, nickel), the absence of an EV industry that would generate demand for the batteries, and social and environmental factors (ECLAC, 2023, p. 23). Resource extraction often occurs in already overstressed eco-systems, e.g., water scarcity in the north of Chile (copper, now lithium) and bauxite and rare earths deposits in the Brazilian Amazon (IEA, 2023). To date, the focus has mainly been on extraction and not on win-win situations to include social and environmental concerns. Johnson et al. (2024) argue that the Chilean state has basically abdicated its responsibility to protect the rights of communities negatively affected by lithium mining in Atacama.

Whether it makes economic sense to try to move up the value chain in lithium or other critical minerals depends on country-specific abilities to address the challenges within a reasonable time horizon. There is considerable uncertainty about how long the window of opportunity will be open given extensive R&D efforts to develop alternatives to critical minerals. Yet, as ECLAC (2023) argues, even if the window is short, the capabilities that could be developed may be transferable.

Beyond Critical Mineral Value Chains

In addition to large reserves of critical minerals, a number of Latin American countries have the right conditions for the generation of green energy. The best solar photovoltaic (PV) conditions are Northern Chile, Peru, and Mexico, and the highest wind potential is in Patagonia (Argentina), the Guajira (Colombia), and Northeastern and Southern Brazil (IEA, 2023).

Some countries also have great potential for hydrogen production, e.g., Argentina, Brazil, Northern Chile, and Mexico. And many countries have hydrogen plans, e.g., Colombia (2021), and Brazil and Chile (2023) (UNIDO, 2024). However, governments have to think carefully about cost and purpose. In an excellent analysis of what we might reasonably expect from hydrogen, Gaster (2024) argues that hydrogen production needs to meet price performance parity (P3) without subsidies if it is to play an important role in addressing global warming. For green hydrogen (derived from green electricity applied to water), around 85 percent of the cost comes from the cost of the electricity input. Consequently, the cost of electricity has to get very low to reach P3. Since transportation costs are high, Gaster suggests that it makes the most sense to co-locate hydrogen use with end uses (e.g., ammonia plants). With respect to blue hydrogen (which uses fossil fuels and carbon capture, utilization, and storage), he maintains that the cost of production will never reach P3.

Another possibility is for governments to leverage increased revenue from critical minerals exports (assuming it is captured in the first place) to diversify the economy in other directions. In the past, industrialization has been the key driver of structural transformation, upgrading, and productivity growth. The confluence of China's competitiveness in industrial products across the spectrum of technology intensity, the rapid change in IT and robotization, and premature de-industrialization in most Latin American countries make it impossible for industrialization to be the single driver of productive transformation and the creation of decent employment.

Countries need a multi-pronged strategy. Although industrialization will continue to be important, the boundaries between manufacturing and other sectors are blurring, and these other sectors will have to play a significant role in future diversification and decarbonization. ECLAC (2024a) identifies key areas with high potential for further diversification and development in the region: renewable energy, sustainable transportation, urban spaces, manufacturing of healthcare, and biochemistry.

The growing application of IT in agriculture has led to 'precision agriculture' in many places, e.g., plants get just the right amount of irrigation and fertilization at the right time, and to the 'industrialization of freshness' (Cramer et al., 2022), the use of sophisticated technologies along the whole supply chain of higher-value agricultural products. Nevertheless, as argued in the introduction, the model of industrial agriculture needs to change, with a greater focus on ecological sustainability and maintenance of biodiversity.

What Role for Foreign Direct Investment in Diversification?

The Asian developing economies which have been most successful in diversification, upgrading, and catching up have used IPs strategically, both green and otherwise (South Korea, Taiwan, China). As part of the process they focused on the creation of national champions using foreign investment and technology where needed. Not surprisingly, scholars of these countries highlight the importance of local ownership for the success of an IP-based strategy, in addition to accountable governance and the right mixture of carrots and sticks and of creation and destruction (Kastelli et al., 2023).

Although there are some national champions and Latin American-owned multinationals *(translatinas)*, multinational corporations (MNCs) have historically played a prominent role in the economic growth and exports of the region. The questions are whether MNCs have an interest in upgrading and diversifying in the host economy, and what the possibilities are for domestic producers to establish linkages with foreign investors and integrate with global value chains. The answers will vary with a country's location-specific assets, the governance structure of global value chains (GVCs), and corporate strategies. Resource- and efficiency-seeking FDI will offer fewer possibilities for upgrading than market- and knowledge-seeking FDI.

Latin American countries with natural resources or propitious climate conditions have attracted resource-seeking FDI, in mineral extraction and agriculture. The governance structure of mining GVCs is hierarchical, and MNCs are primarily interested in exporting the materials with little or no processing. The extent of vertical integration and domestic value added tends to be higher in nationally owned companies than in foreign-owned corporations (Katz & Pietrobelli, 2018). Subsidiaries of foreign companies often only extract locally and process overseas (e.g., in China), while nationally owned companies add more value domestically because they tend to incorporate domestic providers of various subprocesses. In both cases though, there are opportunities for linkages with high-end domestic service providers, as long as they have the requisite knowledge and are willing to assume the risk.

Katz and Pietrobelli (2018, pp. 7–8) highlight the importance of new technology in IT and biochemistry for the development of new services and processes in mining. Some of them have proven to be more environmentally friendly, too, like bioleaching (which uses bacteria to get metal from low-grade ores), e.g., Lithium BioX in Argentina, and rock fragmentation (which reduces costs and has a positive impact on the environment), e.g., EXSA in Peru. For some companies, such linkages have become the springboard for exporting, e.g., mining service providers in Chile (ECLAC, 2024b, p. 250) and service providers linked to renewable energy in Uruguay.

Governments could adopt more aggressive policies to achieve greater localization of the value chain in the host country. Assuming the country has or can develop the requisite knowledge base and infrastructure, MNCs will be more amenable to requirements of localizing if the resource is scarce and expected returns are high. For example, in response to Indonesia's ban on unprocessed nickel exports in 2020, Chinese companies set up huge smelters that turn raw nickel into EV grade battery material. In 2024, Indonesia supplied 61 percent of global refined nickel, up from only 6 percent in 2015 (Lakshmi & Hodgson, 2025). On the other hand, the country's ban on exports of bauxite ore in 2023 had a different outcome. Since the country only has a small share of global production, bauxite companies left (Indonesia Investments, 2023).[10]

Similar opportunities for high-end services (as well as lower-end services) exist in the industrial agro-export sector, with precision agriculture. GVCs for fresh produce are buyer-driven. Large supermarkets in the Global North exert considerable power through the imposition of standards, and they generally prefer to buy from a small number of suppliers with certified standards (Barrett et al., 2022). Upgrading to high-quality products that meet customer demand in the Global North for products which are organic and meet standards of sustainability and social responsibility will add value and command higher prices. But, overall, the potential for linkages is limited. In addition, depending on the crop, inclusion (via increased wages or incorporation of small farmers) tends to be scant, given the large labor pool in the informal sector and MNCs' options to shift production to other locations with suitable climate and soil conditions (Paus et al., 2023).

[10] The US Inflation Reduction Act of 2022 has significant localization requirements, but no requirements regarding the nationality of producers.

Larger Latin American economies have more opportunities to attract market-seeking FDI. Over time, that can generate more possibilities for local linkages and upgrading in manufacturing, especially if the country has a history of manufacturing and offers supporting policies.

The Role of China

In light of China's growing role in Latin America, it is worth taking a closer look at the implications of the country's multifaceted economic interactions with Latin American countries for their ability to upgrade and diversify. Overall, the picture is mixed. On the one hand, trade and investment have exacerbated the commodity dependence of Latin American countries and contributed to premature de-industrialization in the region (Paus, 2020). On the other hand, Chinese investment offers promising opportunities for a green transition and infrastructure expansion.

The dominance of commodities in RR-LAC's exports is even more pronounced for China than the world overall (see Table 2.1). During 2020–2023, copper, copper ores and concentrates, iron ores and concentrates, crude petroleum, and soybeans and other oil seeds accounted for 67 percent of exports to China (Ray et al., 2024, p. 18). In contrast, imports from China consist nearly exclusively of manufactured goods. Where imports from China are cheaper than from other countries, consumers benefit, as do producers for whom the imports are needed inputs. However, China's competitiveness has also undermined manufacturing in LAC (Jenkins, 2014). At times, countries have resorted to protective tariffs, especially in recent years, when China's excess capacity has led to a rapid increase in exports to Latin America (and the rest of the world). For example, between 2014 and 2023, Brazil's imports of steel and iron ore from China increased from $1.6 billion to $2.7 billion (Harris et al., 2024). The Lula Administration responded with an increase in tariffs on different iron and steel products.

If the extraordinarily high tariffs persist that the second Trump Administration imposed on imports from China, and to which China responded in kind, trade diversion will likely intensify RR-LAC's current trade pattern with China. China's soybean imports will further shift from the US to Brazil, Argentina, and Paraguay, while more of China's previous exports will shift to the rest of the world, including RR-LAC. As a result, the pressure on existing manufacturing in RR-LAC will likely intensify.

Table 2.1 RR-LAC's merchandise trade with China and the world, 2022

	Trade balance (millions of US $)		*Chinas' share in country's trade (%)*		*Raw materials as a share of country's exports (%)*		*Distribution of country's goods imports from China (%)*		
	With China	*With world*	*Exports*	*Imports*	*To China*	*TO world*	*Capital goods*	*Cons. goods*	*Intermed. goods*
Argentina	−9573	6923	9	21.5	85	34	51	19	29
Bolivia	−1747	603	5.8	19.4	95	29	35	31	34
Brazil	21,951	42,119	26.8	23.2	90	54	42	15	38
Chile	12,492	−6049	39.5	23.2	52	44	35	46	17
Colombia	−16,545	−20,499	3.8	24.2	69	59	45	24	28
Ecuador	−1038	2331	17.6	22	96	75	38	30	30
Mexico	−107,889	−26,883	1.9	19.6	37	42	52	21	12
Paraguay	−4670	−5931	0.2	29.5	31	49	52	23	24
Peru	1391	−2073	30.1	26.1	80	49	36	34	30
Uruguay	55	−1789	21.5	17.1	89	60	38	35	27
Venezuela	−7391	43,009	0.3	17	57	97	37	24	28

Source: WITS (World Integrated Trade Solution). https://wits.worldbank.org

China is a key player in all stages of the value chain of critical minerals: exploration and production, refining, transport, marketing, and demand. In refining, China accounts for 90 percent of rare earths, 70 percent of cobalt, 50 percent of lithium, and 35 percent of nickel (ECLAC, 2024a, 9). Whether Chinese investors are interested in developing refining capacity in Latin American countries will depend on government requirements and incentives.

Between 2000 and 2023, total Chinese outward foreign direct investment (OFDI) in Latin America amounted to $193.2 billion. Brazil was the primary recipient, with 34 percent, followed by Peru (16.5 percent), Argentina (12.3 percent), Mexico (11.6 percent), and Chile (10.7 percent). Colombia and Venezuela trailed behind, with 3.3 percent and 1.7 percent, respectively (Dussel Peters, 2024, p. 7). While China's OFDI in Latin America used to be concentrated in extractive industries, it has become more diversified in recent years. Chinese investors have positioned themselves in strategic sectors in South America, e.g., digital infrastructure, energy, logistics, and transportation (González Jáuregui & Tussie, 2023). Between 2020 and 2023, Chinese greenfield OFDI in Latin America totaled $21 billion: $12.1 billion in energy, minerals, and mining; $3.2 billion in the automotive sector; $2.2 billion in other manufacturing; $1.2 billion in telecoms and transport; and $2.3 billion in other areas. Mergers and acquisitions added another $25.2 billion (Ray et al., 2024).

Of particular interest is China's possible role in the green transition in Latin America. The country has become the world's largest car exporter and an industrial green powerhouse, with 90 percent of global PV solar capacity and 60 percent of world wind power equipment (Jing, 2024). Its outward investment in clean energy is an initiative across the Global South (White & Sandlund, 2024). In Latin America, Brazil has received the most Chinese investment in developing EVs and infrastructure, while Argentina, Peru and Chile have received the most investment in renewable energy (Ugarteche & García Hernández, 2023). Brazil is also one of the few Latin American countries where Chinese EV producers, e.g., BYD and Great Wall, have localized R&D, production, and sales centers (Myers, 2024).

China's prowess in clean energy production can be a powerful factor in Latin American countries' transition to greater decarbonization. However, currently, governments are not strategic and have not developed a joint agenda in their interactions with China so as to realize the role that Chinese investment could play in diversifying and greening the region.

Instead countries compete with each other to attract FDI from China (Gonzalez-Jauregui and Tussie, 2023).

Concluding Thoughts

In this chapter I have argued for the critical importance of government leadership to adopt and implement IPs for the implementation of an IGD strategy. There are a number of other important areas that need attention to increase the likelihood of IP success in Latin American countries. But, in the absence of leadership and continuity over time, governments cannot take advantage of the window of opportunity that the demand for critical minerals offers.

It is important to remember that even with political leadership and a cohesive industrial strategy, the new areas of dynamic comparative advantage are not likely to generate sufficient decent employment opportunities. To that end, governments will also need to devise policies that focus on improving conditions for SMEs, for workers in the informal sector, and, more broadly, for non-tradeable services (Rodrik & Stiglitz, 2024; Paus, 2025).

References

Agosin, M. (2023). Productive development policy for Chile: An alternative to stagnation. *CEPAL Review, 139*, 117–133.

Amsden, A. (2001). *The rise of the rest. Challenges to the West from late-industrializing economies.* Oxford University Press.

Andreoni, A. (2017). Varieties of industrial policy: Models, packages and transformation cycles. In A. Noman & J. Stiglitz (Eds.), *Efficiency, finance and varieties of industrial policy* (pp. 245–305). Columbia University Press.

Anzolin, G., & Lebdioui, A. (2021). Three dimensions of green industrial policy in the context of climate Change and sustainable Development. *The European Journal of Development Research, 33*, 371–405. https://doi.org/10.1057/s41287-021-00365-5

Barrett, C. B., Reardon, T., Swinnen, J., & Zilberman, D. (2022). Agri-food value chain revolutions in low- and middle-income countries. *Journal of Economic Literature, 60*(4), 1316–1377. https://doi.org/10.1257/jel.20201539

Becker Toro, R. (2024). *El esquivo desarrollo de la industria de litio para Chile.* Wilson Center. Latin America Program.

Benites Lazaro, L. L., & Serrani, E. (2023). Conclusions: Energy transition agenda for sustainable development in Latin America. In L. L. Benites Lazaro

& E. Serrani (Eds.), *Energy transitions in Latin America. The tough road to sustainable development* (pp. 437–355). Springer.

Bergquist, P., Mildenberger, M., & Stokes, L. C. (2020). Combining climate, economic and social policy builds public support for climate action in the US. *Environmental Research Letters, 15*(5), 054019.

BID. (2024). *Síntesis de información y datos sobre integración y comercio.* Connexa. No 23.

Block, F. (2008). Swimming against the current: The rise of a hidden developmental state in the United States. *Politics and Society, 36*(2), 169–206. https://doi.org/10.1177/0032329208318731

Bril-Mascarenhas, T., & Madariaga, A. (2019). Business power and the minimal state: The defeat of industrial policy in Chile. *The Journal of Development Studies, 55*(6), 1047–1066. https://doi.org/10.1080/00220388.2017.1417587

Castillo, M., & Ominami, C. (2024). Transformación productiva y nueva actualidad de las políticas industriales en América Latina. *Estudios Internacionales.* Universidad de Chile, *207*, 185–216.

Chang, H. J. (2003). *Kicking away the ladder.* Anthem Press.

Cherif, R., & Hasanov, F. (2019). *The return of the policy that shall not be named: Principles of industrial policy* (IMF working paper 2019/74).

Cimoli, G., Dosi, & Stiglitz, J. (2009). *Industrial policy and development: The political economy of capabilities accumulation.* Oxford University Press.

Cramer, C., DiJohn, J., & Sender, J. (2022). Classification and roundabout production in high-value agriculture: A fresh approach to industrialization. *Development and Change, 53*, 495–524. https://doi.org/10.1111/dech.12708

Dechezleprêtre, A., et al. (2025). Fighting climate change: International attitudes toward climate policies. *American Economic Review, 115*(4), 1258–1300. https://doi.org/10.1257/aer.20230501

DiPippo, G., Mazzocco, I., & Kennedy, S. (2022). *Red ink. Estimating Chinese industrial policy spending in comparative perspective.* Center for Strategic and International Studies.

Dussel Peters, E. (2024). China OFDI in Latin America and the Caribbean 2024. *Red ALC-China.* https://docs.dusselpeters.com/395.pdf

ECLAC. (2023). *Lithium extraction and industrialization. Opportunities and challenges for Latin America and the Caribbean.* Economic Commission on Latin America and the Caribbean.

ECLAC. (2024a). *Panorama of productive development policies in Latin America and the Caribbean.* Executive Summary. LC/PUB.2024/17.

ECLAC. (2024b). *Natural resources outlook in Latin America and the Caribbean, 2023.* Economic Commission for Latin America and the Caribbean.

Evenett, S., et al. (2024). *The return of industrial policy in data.* International Monetary Fund. https://thedocs.worldbank.org/en/doc/7476416e217a50134c0570af1a3f8e5b-0370012024/original/PPT-NIPO-Spillovers.pdf

Fagerberg, J., & Srholec, M. (2008). National innovation systems, capabilities, and economic development. *Research Policy, 37*, 1417–1435. https://doi.org/10.1016/j.respol.2008.06.003

Gallagher, K. (2016). *The China triangle. Latin America's China boom and the fate of the Washington Consensus.* Oxford University Press.

Gaster, R. 2024. A realist approach to hydrogen. Information Technology & Innovation Foundation. https://itif.org/publications/2024/01/16/a-realist-approach-to-hydrogen/

González Jáuregui, J. (2024). *La presencia de China en el sector del litio en Argentina.* Wilson Center. Latin America Program.

González Jáuregui, J., & Tussie, D. (2023). La presencia económica de China en Sudamérica: Implicaciones para las dinámicas de cooperación intraregional. *URVIO Revista Latinoamericana de Estudios de Seguridad, 36*, 8–25.

Griffith-Jones, S., & Ocampo, J. A. (2018). *The future of national development banks.* Oxford University Press.

Hamrin, O. (2024). *The Silicon Empire: TSMC's revolution and Morris Chang's legacy.* https://quartr.com/insights/company-research/the-silicon-empire-tsmcs-revolution-and-morris-changs-legacy

Harris, B., Leahy, J., & Lakshmi, A. (2024, March 17). Brazil launches China anti-dumping probe after imports soar. *Financial Times.*

Hausmann, R., Hwang, J., & Rodrik, D. (2007). What you export matters. *Journal of Economic Growth, 12*, 1–25. https://doi.org/10.1007/s10887-006-9009-4

Healy, A., & Malhotra, N. (2009). Myopic voters and natural disaster policy. *American Political Science Review, 103*(3), 387–406. https://doi.org/10.1017/S0003055409990104

Heywood, J. (1546). *A dialogue conteinyng the nomber in effect of all the prouerbes in the Englishe tongue.*

Hufbauer, G., & Jung, E. (2021). Scoring 50 years of US industrial policy, 1970–2020. *PIIE briefing 21-5*, Peterson Institute for International Economics.

IEA (International Energy Agency). (2023). *Latin America Energy Outlook.* www.iea.org

Indonesia Investments. (2023). *Bauxite ore export ban: Developing a domestic mineral refining & processing industry in Indonesia.* https://www.indonesia-investments.com/news/news-columns/bauxite-ore-export-ban-developing-a-domestic-mineral-refining-processing-industry-in-indonesia/item9638?#:~:text=On%2010%20June%202023%20the,move%20was%20not%20a%20surprise

Javorcik, B. et al. (2023, November 21). *The green transition and geopolitical tensions.* VOXEU.

Jenkins, R. (2014). Chinese competition and Brazilian exports of manufactures. *Oxford Development Studies, 42*(3), 395–418. https://doi.org/10.1080/13600818.2014.881989

Jing, B. (2024). A study of China-Latin America cooperation in green energy industry: Status, obstacles and the policy suggestions. *International Journal of Sustainable Development and Planning, 19*(6), 2381–2393. https://doi.org/10.18280/ijsdp.190636n

Johnson, C., Clavijo, A., Lorca, M., & Oliveira Andrade, M. (2024). Bringing the state back in the lithium triangle: An institutional analysis of resource nationalism in Chile, Argentina, and Bolivia. *The Extractive Industries and Society, 20.* https://doi.org/10.1016/j.exis.2024.101534

Juhász, R., & Lane, N. L. (2024). The political economy of industrial policy. *The Journal of Economic Perspectives, 38*(4), 27–54. https://doi.org/10.1257/jep.38.4.27

Juhász, R., Lane, N., Oehlsen, E., Pérez, V.C. (2023a). *The who, what, when, and how of industrial policy: A text-based approach.* https://osf.io/preprints/socarxiv/uyxh9

Juhász, R., Lane, N., & Rodrik, D. (2023b). *The new economics of industrial policy* (NBER working paper 31538).

Kastelli, I., Mamica, L., & Lee, K. (2023). New perspectives and issues in industrial policy for sustainable development: From developmental and entrepreneurial state to environmental state. *Review of Evolutionary Political Economy, 4*, 1–25. https://doi.org/10.1007/s43253-023-00100-2

Katz, J., & Pietrobelli, C. (2018). Natural resource based growth, global value chains and domestic capabilities in the mining industry. *Resources Policy, 58*, 11–20. https://doi.org/10.1016/j.resourpol.2018.02.001

Kemp, R., & Never, B. (2017). Green transition, industrial policy, and economic development. *Oxford Review of Economic Policy, 33*(1), 66–84. https://doi.org/10.1093/oxrep/grw037

Lakshmi, A., & Hodgson, C. (2025, February 12). The Opec of Nickel': Indonesia's control of a critical mineral. *Financial Times.*

Lebdioui, A. (2024). *Survival of the greenest. Economic transformation in a climate-conscious world.* UNU WIDER and Cambridge University Press. https://doi.org/10.1017/9781009339414

Lin, J., & Chang, H. J. (2009). Should industrial policy in developing countries conform to comparative advantage or defy it? A debate between Justin Lin and Ha-Joon Chang. *Development and Policy Review, 27*(5_), 483–502. https://doi.org/10.1111/j.1467-7679.2009.00456.x

Mazzucato, M. (2013). *The entrepreneurial state.* Anthem Press.

Mazzucato, M. (2024, January 19). *A progressive green growth narrative*. Project Syndicate.

Mazzucato, M., & Monaco, L. (2024). Rethinking industrial strategies and the state: A Global South perspective. *Social Research. An International Quarterly, 91*(3), 819–849. https://doi.org/10.1353/sor.2024.a938579

Mazzucato, M., & Rodrik, D. (2024). *Industrial policy with conditionalities: A taxonomy and sample cases* (Working paper WP2023/07, updated April 2024). Institute for Innovation and Public Purpose.

Meadows, S. (2023, December 27). Uruguay's green power revolution: Rapid shift to wind shows the world how it is done. *The Guardian*.

Méndez Galain, R. (2023). *TED talk*. https://www.youtube.com/watch?v=7_3XJhFBvEk

Milanez, B., & Dorn, F. M. (2024). Lithium policies in Latin America: Old wine in new bottles? *Extractivism policy brief no.8*. www.extractivism.de

Myers, M. (2024, June 21). China's EV drive accelerates in Latin America. *East Asia Forum*. https://eastasiaforum.org/2024/06/21/chinas-ev-drive-accelerates-in-latin-america/

Ocampo, J. A. (2017). Dynamic efficiency. Structural dynamics and economic growth in developing countries. In A. Noman & J. Stiglitz (Eds.), *Efficiency, finance and varieties of industrial policy* (pp. 65–102). Columbia University Press.

Ocampo, J. A., Rada, C., & Taylor, L. (2009). *Growth and policy in developing countries. A structuralist approach*. Columbia University Press.

Oqubay, A., Cramer, C., Chang, H., & Kozul-Wright, R. (2020). *Oxford handbook of industrial policy*. Oxford University Press.

Oreiro, J. L. (2024, September 4–6). Class coalition and the political economy of New Developmentalism: An essay in honour of Bresser-Pereira. In *Paper prepared for the 36th conference of the European association for evolutionary political economy*, Bilbao.

Paus, E. (2005). *Foreign investment, development, and globalization. Can Costa Rica become Ireland*. Palgrave Macmillan.

Paus, E. (2020). Innovation strategies matter: Latin America's middle income trap meets China and globalisation. *The Journal of Development Studies, 56*(4). https://doi.org/10.1080/00220388.2019.1595600

Paus, E. (2025). What role for modern services in Latin America's economic development? In A. K. Dutt, N. Lustig, J. C. Moreno Brid, & J. A. Ocampo (Eds.), *Economic development, economic growth and income distribution: Structuralist perspectives on Latin America and beyond* (pp. 142–167). Edward Elgar Publishing.

Paus, E., Abugattas, L., & Cruz-Saco, M. A. (2023). Global value chains in agriculture and the middle-income trap: A framework for analysis applied to Peru's boom. *The Journal of Development Studies, 59*, 1531–1548. https://doi.org/10.1080/00220388.2023.2232919

Ponce, J. C. (2024). Uruguay, pioneer in renewable energy: A model for the world? *Yale Climate Connections*. https://yaleclimateconnections.org/2024/12/uruguay-pioneer-in-renewable-energy-a-model-for-the-world/

Ray, R., Albright, Z. A., & Dussel Peters, E. (2024). *China-Latin America and the Caribbean Economic Bulletin* (2024th ed.). Global Development Policy Center, Boston University.

Reilly, T. (2024). African raw material export bans: Protectionism or self-determination? *Global Policy Watch*. https://www.globalpolicywatch.com/2024/05/african-raw-material-export-bans-protectionism-or-self-determination/

Rodrik, D., & Stiglitz, J. (2024). A new growth strategy for developing nations. Copy at https://tinyurl.com/ymrg8qom

Stiglitz, J., & Lin, J. Y. (Eds.). (2013). *The industrial policy revolution I. The role of government beyond ideology*. Palgrave Macmillan.

Studwell, J. (2013). *How Asia works. Success and failure in the world's most dynamic region*. Grove Press.

Sullivan, J. (2023). *Remarks by National Security Advisor Jake Sullivan on Renewing American Economic Leadership at the Brookings Institution*. https://www.whitehouse.gov/briefing-room/speeches-remarks/2023/04/27/remarks-by-national-security-advisor-jake-sullivan-on-renewing-american-economic-leadership-at-the-brookings-institution/

Tagliapietra, S., & Veugelers, R. (2021). Fostering the industrial component of the European Green Deal: Key principles and policy options. *Intereconomics, 56*(6). https://doi.org/10.1007/s10272-021-1006-5

Thurbon, E., Kim, S. Y., Tan, H., & Mathews, J. (2023). *Developmental environmentalism*. Oxford University Press.

Ugarteche, O., & García Hernández, J. (2023). Energy matrix transformation in Latin America: The global political economy of Chinese investments. In L. L. Benites Lazaro & E. Serrani (Eds.), *Energy transitions in Latin America. The tough road to sustainable development* (pp. 59–78). Springer.

UNIDO. (2024). *Industrial development report 2024*. United Nations Industrial Development Organization.

Wade, R. (2018). *Governing the market: Economic theory and the role of government in East Asian industrialization*. Princeton University Press.

Weiss, J., & Seric, A. (2020). Industrial policy: Clarifying options through taxonomy and decision trees. *Development and Policy Review, 39*, 773–788. https://doi.org/10.1111/dpr.12522

White, E., & Sandlund, W. (2024, October 1). Chinese outbound investment surges to record on clean energy 'Tsunami.' *Financial Times*.

Yülek, M., et al. (2020). State capacity and the role of industrial policy in automobile industry: A comparative analysis of Turkey and South Korea. *Journal of Industry, Competition and Trade, 20*, 307–331. https://doi.org/10.1016/j.respol.2008.06.003

CHAPTER 3

Maximizing Policy and Fiscal Space for an Inclusive Green Strategy

Eva Paus

Abstract Latin American governments need to have the requisite policy and fiscal space to implement an inclusive green development strategy. In this chapter, I analyze two important factors which impact that space significantly: the commitments and demands under international trade and investment agreements, and the financial resources available to achieve the desired goals. I propose possible actions to broaden the space, both at the international and the national level. Internationally, the rules need to be made compatible with the Sustainable Development Goals, and thus with the implementation of an inclusive green transition, and financial resources for a green transition have to grow considerably. Nationally, governments can expand policy space by terminating international investment agreements which include an investor-state dispute settlement mechanism. And they can increase fiscal space in several ways, importantly—in the current context—by appropriating a larger share of the natural resource rent.

Keywords Policy space • Fiscal space • International trade and investment treaties • Investor-state dispute settlement mechanism • Natural resource rents • International financial architecture • Tax reform • WTO

E. Paus, R. Domínguez, *Toward Inclusive Development in Latin America*, Palgrave Studies in Latin American Heterodox Economics, https://doi.org/10.1007/978-3-032-08588-7_3

We have all the tools and resources to solve our shared challenges. What we need is determination.
—António Guterres, Secretary General of the United Nations[1]

Latin American governments need to have policy and fiscal space to implement an IGD strategy. In this chapter, I focus on two important factors circumscribing that space: (1) the commitments and demands under international trade and investment agreements, and (2) the financial resources available to achieve the desired goals. I propose possible actions to broaden the space, both at the international and the national level. Internationally, the rules need to be made compatible with the Sustainable Development Goals, and thus with the implementation of an inclusive green transition, and financial resources for a green transition in Latin America have to grow considerably. Nationally, governments can expand policy space by terminating international investment agreements which include an investor-state dispute settlement mechanism. And they can increase fiscal space in several ways, importantly—in the current context—by appropriating a larger share of the natural resource rent.

Tackling International Trade and Investment-Linked Constraints

International trade and investment agreements and policies have constrained national policy space in three important ways: (1) the paradigm change in the international trading system with the move from the General Agreement on Tariffs and Trade (GATT) to the World Trade Organization (WTO); (2) the inclusion of an investor-state-dispute-settlement (ISDS) mechanism in many trade and investment agreements; and (3) a growing number of unilateral trade policies by developed countries on the basis of national security or the green transition. Below, I analyze each of them in turn.

[1]Address to the General Assembly, September 19, 2023, https://www.un.org/sg/en/content/sg/speeches/2023-09-19/secretary-generals-address-the-general-assembly.

From the GATT to the WTO: Restrictions of Policy Space

With the exception of Ecuador, the RR-LAC were all members of the GATT, a multilateral agreement signed in 1947 to regulate international trade after WWII.[2] During successive negotiation rounds tariffs were reduced progressively. The Uruguay Round (1986–1994) gave rise to the establishment of the WTO, which incorporated the GATT and dramatically changed the rules governing global trade among its members. Although the WTO maintained the most favored nation (MFN) principle, a cornerstone of the GATT, it presented a major paradigm shift (Shadlen, 2006; Abugattas & Paus, 2008; Thrasher, 2021).

First, developing countries were no longer accorded special and differential treatment (S&DT), except for least developed countries. S&DT had been grounded in preferential market access, flexibility in how disciplines were applied, and, generally, non-reciprocal trade relations between developed and developing countries. As a result, under the GATT, developing countries had considerable leeway in their choice of development policies and strategies. Under the WTO, in contrast, all countries have to abide by the same rules and have the same obligations.

The second major shift was the broadening of the trade-related agenda to incorporate subsidies (Agreement on Subsidies and Countervailing Measures, ASCM), intellectual property rights (Trade-Related Intellectual Property Rights, TRIPs), and investment (Trade-Related Investment Measures, TRIMs). These agreements are part of a single undertaking, i.e., members have to accept all of them. The WTO expansion into services (General Agreement on Trade in Services, GATS), on the other hand, is based on a positive list, where members decide which disciplines to include. And the Government Procurement Agreement is a plurilateral agreement, where WTO members opt in or not.

The broadening of the agenda significantly reduced the policy space for developing countries (see Table 3.1 for details). Important measures that advanced development in the past are no longer permitted, e.g., key performance requirements for foreign investors and export subsidies. With the WTO rules, industrialized countries effectively "kicked away the ladder" (Chang, 2002).

[2] Brazil and Chile were among the 23 founding members of the GATT. All countries transitioned from the GATT to the WTO in 1995; Ecuador joined in 1996.

Table 3.1 Policy space under WTO agreements

	Measures permitted	*Limitations*
General		
Possibilities for exclusion		Single undertaking, none
Tariff limits	Country can raise applied tariff to bound tariff rate	Country cannot exceed bound tariffs
GATT Article XI	Export taxes	Quantitative restrictions on exports
GATT Article XX(b)	Measures necessary for environmental and other public interest protection	
GATT Article XX (e)	Measures related to exhaustible natural resources	
GATT Article XXI	National security exception	
GATT Article XXIV	Allows for preferential and regional trade agreements as long as they are liberalizing	
Additional Agreements		
Agreement on Subsidies and Countervailing Measures (ASCM), only applies to goods	General subsidies; drawbacks; compensation of higher capital cost; subsidies for R&D; human capital development; export subsidies that fall under the *de minimis* clause	Specific subsidies (enterprise, industry,[a] region); subsidies for exports; subsidies for local content
Trade-related Investment Measures (TRIMs), only applies to goods	Require technology transfer from foreign investors Demand joint ventures Restrictions on foreign firms in particular sectors	Performance requirements, incl. Local content requirements (i.e., requirements to establish backward linkages); requirements to sell in local market; trade balancing; foreign exchange restrictions
Trade-related Intellectual Property (TRIPs), only applies to goods	Compulsory licenses (use patented products w/o the permission of patent owner), e.g., health crisis, national emergency	Patent terms shorter than 20 years; patent recognition is mandatory
General Agreement on Trade in Services (GATS)	Positive list; countries opt in to market access and national treatment commitments; Subsidies for service exports	Negative list approach to MFN treatment

(*continued*)

Table 3.1 (continued)

	Measures permitted	*Limitations*
Government Procurement Agreement	Public procurement	Plurilateral Agreement, applicable only to member parties

[a]Industry subsidies are not prohibited, but actionable. Burden of proof is on country that feels negatively impacted

Nonetheless, governments in LAC (and elsewhere) can still take a number of actions under WTO rules (see Table 3.1). With respect to ASCM, for example, Agosin (2023) argues that Chile can subsidize new exports until they reach $50 million, a sum that is likely to fall under the *de minimis* clause.[3] Government procurement can be an important tool for creating a market for new domestically produced products; and none of the Latin American countries is party to the Government Procurement Agreement. The measures permitted under the TRIMs agreement are particularly relevant given the prominence of multinational companies in Latin America. They include requiring technology transfer, demanding joint ventures, and restricting foreign investment in specific sectors.

The third major change in the shift from the GATT to the WTO was the establishment of a two-step Dispute Settlement Mechanism (DSM), which allows for the enforcement of rules. That is especially important for smaller countries which otherwise have little recourse to fair treatment in a world where big powers dominate. If a country believes that a trading partner is violating WTO rules, it can bring a case before a WTO panel.[4] If one of the parties does not agree with the panel's ruling, it can appeal to the Appellate Body of the WTO, whose ruling is then final and binding.

Since the wording of WTO rules can be broad and subject to interpretation, the Appellate Body decides which rule prevails when they are in conflict with each other. Especially important for a green transition is GATT Article XX(b), which allows for measures necessary to protect the environment and other public interests. Yet, when it is implemented in a

[3]The clause states that an importing country can only take action if imports from a specific country exceed two percent of imports of the importing country.

[4]Of course, violations of WTO rules only have consequences if they are challenged. Fuel subsidies, for example, are not allowed under the ASCM, but they have not been challenged.

way that conflicts with other rules, the Appellate Body has tended to rule against environmental protection (Thrasher, 2017; Lebdioui, 2024).

The DSM has been non-functioning since 2017, when the Trump Administration started blocking appointments of new members.[5] The implications for developing countries are ambiguous. On the one hand, it opens policy space for developing countries (Hopewell, 2024), a space which Indonesia, for example, used when it appealed the WTO decision in favor of the EU challenge of Indonesia's ban on raw nickel exports.[6] On the other hand, it does not allow countries to seek remedy for WTO rule violations. Weighing greater policy space against a functioning dispute settlement process, a group of WTO members established a Multi-Party Interim Appeal Arbitration Arrangement in 2020, with the rulings applying only to participating countries. Several Latin American countries joined the Arrangement, including Brazil, Chile, Colombia, Mexico, Peru, and Uruguay.

Over the past decades, many Latin American governments have signed a slew of bilateral and regional trade and investment agreements, which significantly reduced the policy space remaining under the WTO. While the specifics vary by country, these agreements generally incorporate and restrict areas beyond those covered under the WTO, e.g., government procurement, investment, competition, environments, sectors covered by GATS, national treatment of foreign investors, and drawbacks (Shadlen, 2006). And in areas already covered by the WTO, bilateral and regional agreements often enshrine even deeper commitments. However, regional agreements among LAC have not significantly infringed upon countries' policy space, since enforcement mechanisms are limited, and there is greater flexibility (Abugattas & Paus, 2008).

The main motivation behind the 'spaghetti bowl' of agreements has always been market access; and, once a certain number of countries have signed bilateral agreements, pressure increases on others not to be left out. But market access comes at a high price, as policy space has shrunk even more.

[5] Since 2020, all seven positions have been unfilled, and the Biden Administration followed Trump in blocking appointments.

[6] It is ironic that after a WTO panel sided with China's challenge of the first Trump Administration's tariffs on steel and aluminum as not justified on national security grounds, the Biden Administration appealed to the very Appellate Body which their actions had rendered impotent.

In recent years, there have been increasing calls for reforming the WTO so as to bring the rules in line with the need and ability to achieve the Sustainable Development Goals (Thrasher, 2021; Sasmal, 2024). Such reforms are challenging, since there are different interest groups, and developed countries generally have little interest in changing rules that benefit them. However, RR-LAC governments have control at the national level. They need to assess whether violation of WTO rules in pursuit of inclusive green development can be justified on national security grounds (see Chap. 2). And they would do well to review their bilateral trade agreements to determine whether the agreed upon constraints are worth the development costs.

ISDS: Unique Privileges for Foreign Investors Limit Policy Space

One of the policy space limitations with particularly wide-ranging consequences and costs is the inclusion of an investor-state-dispute-settlement (ISDS) mechanism in international trade and investment agreements. ISDS is a private dispute settlement mechanism which allows foreign investors to bring claims against host country governments before a private international tribunal in a country of their choice. The ability of an investor to sue a sovereign state outside the host country's jurisdiction is unique under international law.[7] It creates an uneven playing field in favor of multinational corporations (MNCs) and against governments and national investors. MNCs have rights, but no obligations: only they can bring claims, not the host country government; they can shop around for the arbitration forum which suits them best; and there is no transparency about the rulings.

Investment treaties guarantee foreign investors protection of their investments in the host country. They typically include compensation for direct or indirect expropriations, for treatment that is not 'equal and fair,' and for discrimination. Governments sign international investment agreements in the expectation that they will increase foreign direct investment (FDI) inflows. And FDI—in turn—is expected to contribute to the country's economic development, be it through an increase in capital, creation

[7] The WTO only allows states to bring claims against other states; and in international human rights courts, claimants have to exhaust domestic venues before taking disputes outside the country (Rangel et al., 2023).

of new jobs, generation of foreign exchange, or technological spillovers to domestic producers.

However, the empirical evidence in support of these expectations is mixed, both with respect to the impact of FDI on economic development and the impact of international investment agreements on the magnitude of FDI. The impact of FDI on development depends on the nature of FDI (resource-seeking, efficiency-seeking, market-seeking, knowledge-seeking) as well as on the ability of developing countries to absorb technological spillovers and create linkages to the production of foreign investors in the country (Paus, 2005). In a meta-analysis of 40 articles, Goerg and Greenaway (2004) conclude that "robust empirical evidence for positive spillovers is at best mixed." And, as discussed in Chap. 2, domestic producers may find it difficult to upgrade in GVCs.

Literature surveys on the impact of bilateral investment treaties on FDI inflows indicate that the empirical evidence is also mixed at best (Aisbett et al., 2018; Reiter & Bellak, 2020; Brada et al., 2021). Against these uncertain benefits are the well-documented costs of including ISDS in treaties.

In early 2025, nearly 400 bilateral and multilateral investment agreements (IIAs) were in force in the RR-LAC. The number of IIAs varies considerably by country, with Argentina and Chile at the high end of the spectrum and Brazil, Bolivia, and Ecuador at the low end (Table 3.2). While Brazil has always been skeptical of the benefits of IIAs, Bolivia and Ecuador terminated most of their IIAs during the 2010s. Countries also differ in the inclusion of ISDS in IIAs. Brazil is the only country with no ISDS, and Bolivia and Ecuador have only one IIA with ISDS. For the other countries, over 70 percent of IIAs include ISDS (Table 3.2). Looking at RR-LAC's most important trading partners, we find that the US has an IIA with all countries except Bolivia, Ecuador, Paraguay, and Venezuela, and they all include ISDS save for the one with Brazil (data not shown in table). China has an IIA with all countries except Bolivia, Brazil, Paraguay, and Venezuela; they all incorporate ISDS with the exception of Chile and Ecuador. None of the multilateral agreements with the EU include ISDS.

Of the 321 cases brought against the RR-LAC by February 2025, 48 percent have been concluded, with slightly more than half decided in favor of the investor; 12.5 percent resulted in settlements, 9.7 percent were discontinued, and 31.5 percent are still pending (see Table 3.2) Nearly 90 percent of the cases have been brought by investors from developed

Table 3.2 International investment treaties in force and ISDS cases and solutions

	IIAs in force				*ISDS cases brought against Latin American host country*							
	Total	*With ISDS*	*W/o ISDS*	*No data*	*Total*	*Decided in favor of*			*Settled*	*Discontinued or suspended*	*Pending*	*Total awarded & settled*[a] *(in current US $)*
						Investor	*State*	*Neither or no data*				
Argentina	62	52	9	1	65	23	7	1	16	11	7	$9,223,621,417
Bolivia	6	1	5		19	5	2		10	1	1	$1,151,590,000
Brazil	17		17									
Chile	64	41	23		7	2	3				2	$15,800,000
Colombia	23	16	7		24	2	6	1		1	14	$28,500,000
Ecuador	7	1	6		34	12	7		3	4	13	$2,176,541,279
Mexico	47	41	6		52	11	12		1	6	22	$289,840,000
Paraguay	37	25	12		3	1	1		1			$60,000,000
Peru	49	40	9		49	6	12	1	2	3	25	$232,431,202
Uruguay	46	33	13		5	1	4					$60,000,000
Venezuela	29	23	4	2	63	19	15		7	5	17	$16,010,042,292
Total	387	273	111	3	321	82	69	3	40	31	101	$29,248,366,190

Source: Author's calculations based on Georgetown Law, Center for the Advancement of the Rule of Law in the Americas, Investment Agreements Database, accessed February 15, 2025

[a]Most settled cases do not disclose the amount settled for; thus the total including all settled amounts is higher than shown here.

countries. US MNCs accounted for 28 percent, followed by Spain with 15 percent, and Canada with 9 percent. In contrast, China has brought only two cases, which may be due to Chinese firms' strong preference for consultation and negotiation (Du, 2023). Nearly 90 percent of cases were arbitrated under the International Center for the Settlement of Investment Disputes (ICSID), which was established in 1961 under the auspices of the World Bank. Brazil was never a member of ICSID; Bolivia, Venezuela, and Ecuador withdrew, but Ecuador rejoined in 2021 under the Lasso government.

Among the small number of companies from developing countries which brought cases against RR-LAC governments are 11 cases brought by Peruvian firms against their own government. Peruvian law allows Peruvian firms to include ISDS in contracts with and concessions from the government. If the reason for this extraordinary provision is weakness of the domestic court system, then policies might be better focused on strengthening the judicial system than offering ISDS options to domestic firms.

ISDS imposes serious constraints on the policy space needed for an inclusive green strategy (Rangel et al., 2023; Müller & Ghiotto, 2024). First, treaty language is generally vague, with reference to 'fair and equitable treatment' and 'indirect expropriation.' That gives arbitration panels considerable leeway in interpreting any host country measure impacting a company's actual or projected profitability as violating obligations to the foreign investor.

Cases that foreign investors have brought against developing country governments in Latin America and elsewhere illustrate the severity of the threat to a progressive agenda. They include challenges to efforts to reduce tax evasion and to strengthen environmental laws, responses to climate change and to reduce fossil fuel extraction, regulations of the price and quality of essential public services and of healthcare services, and intellectual property rights that balance public and private needs (Rangel et al., 2023, pp. 4–5).

In Latin America, examples of ISDS actions against public interest policies abound: Chevron (US) v. Ecuador over cleaning up the environmental damages from oil drilling; Red Eagle (Canada) v. Colombia over lost profits after banning mining to protect the Paramos which provides 85 percent of the country's water supply; GMS Gas (US) v. Argentina over the country's macro stabilization efforts in 2001; and Odyssey Marine

Exploration (US) v. Mexico over the denial of a permit for mining in the Gulf of Ulloa (Public Citizen, 2024).

Second, ISDS can have a regulatory chill on government actions, where governments do not take needed measures out of fear of an ISDS suit. For example, when Peru's congress passed a law in April 2020 to suspend highway tolls during the pandemic, the government itself challenged the law before the highest court fearing the financial costs of possible ISDS claims (Rangel et al., 2023, p. 17).

Third, the amounts awarded to MNCs can be staggering, e.g., Conoco Phillips (Netherlands) v. Venezuela—$8.4 billion; Burlington Resources (US) v. Ecuador—$397.8 million; and Argentina settled with Repsol (Spain) for $5 billion. The totals for all countries add up to nearly $30 billion (see Table 3.2). Even when an arbitration panel rules in favor of the state, the government does not win, it just does not lose. And even then, the process involves a significant amount of time and money. It may take several years and even decades before a case is finally concluded; and the average arbitration cost is estimated at $4.7 million (Rangel et al., 2023).

Two Latin American governments unilaterally cancelled their bilateral investment treaties (BITs) in response to popular outrage over ISDS cases: the privileges they give to foreign investors and high awards to foreign investors. Bolivia, under Morales, was the first Latin American country to leave the ICSID Convention in 2007; and the country's 2009 constitution mandates that foreign investors use the domestic judicial system for any claims. By 2013, the government had terminated all its 22 BITs. In Ecuador, the cancellation of BITs proceeded in two waves under Correa: 2008–2010 and 2017–2018. When the Noboa Administration proposed renewed inclusion of ISDS in IIAs in a referendum (April 2024), the population rejected it resoundingly (Mehranvar et al., 2024).

There is growing agreement that the ISDS system needs to change, especially since the number of claims have exploded in recent years, not least due to the increasing participation of third-party funding hedge funds and financiers (Greenfield & Weston, 2025). Proposals generally tinker with the structure, but do not address the fundamental problem of allowing a private foreign investor to sue a sovereign state outside the host country's jurisdiction. They include the proposals by the United Nations Commission on International Trade Law Working Group III (e.g., inclusion of the possibility for counterclaims), the EU pushing for a standing international court, and other proposals with more obligations for investors, greater regulatory space for host country governments, and more third-party rights in disputes.[8]

The only real solution is to withdraw consent and terminate the treaty, the path taken by Ecuador and Bolivia. Other Latin American countries need to seriously consider this option, because it opens critically needed policy space. It is true that IIAs generally include sunset clauses, which means that the treaty remains in effect for the number of years specified in the treaty for investments made prior to the cancelation date. But retention of ISDS leaves open the possibility of claims into the indefinite future. Furthermore, evidence suggests that termination of BITs has not had a negative impact on FDI inflows (Public Citizen, 2018; Mehranvar et al., 2024).

The most effective way to get rid of the ISDS regime may be rejection on a multilateral basis. In recent years, governments in developed economies have taken this route in several instances, e.g., EU member states withdrew from the EU Energy Charter, and the US and Canada eliminated ISDS between themselves in the United States-Mexico-Canada Agreement and limited its scope with respect to Mexico. The Americas Partnership for Economic Prosperity (APEP) could have been the locus for terminating ISDS on a broad scale in the Western Hemisphere (Rangel et al., 2023), but that is unlikely to happen under the second Trump Administration. Nonetheless, Latin American governments could start by revising or canceling the considerable number of BITs they have among themselves.

Unilateral Trade Measures in the Global North: The Latest Challenge

The latest challenges to governments' policy space stem from measures by the second Trump Administration which disregard established rules, and from new EU rules aimed at advancing the green transition in Europe and elsewhere. Chapter 5 discusses the implications of the Trump Administration's policies in the larger context of changing global

[8] Under Brazil's Cooperation and Facilitation Investment Agreement Model, foreign investors have to follow institutional mechanisms that aim to promote cooperation and avoid arbitration. And South Africa, which also terminated most of its BITs, changed the arbitration regime to allow for state-to-state arbitration, but only after foreign investors have exhausted the domestic channels for dispute settlement (Duarte & Rangel, 2023).

geopolitical and economic power constellations, with the rivalry between China and the US at its core. Here, I focus briefly on the EU's carbon border adjustment measure (CBAM) and deforestation regulation, neither of which includes exceptions for developing countries.

The CBAM is a carbon tax on imported goods which is intended to address potential 'carbon leakage,' i.e., if the EU has stricter emissions regulations than other countries, EU companies may relocate. It covers iron, steel, cement, aluminum, hydrogen, and electricity. Under the CBAM, exporters to the EU have to purchase emission permits, and thus pay a price for the CO_2 embedded in the exports, "...equivalent to the CO_2 emitted when producing under the EU's emissions trading system" (Weinhardt & De Ville, 2024).

Latin American countries will be affected to varying degrees. The share of exports to the EU of the products involved are 45 percent for Venezuela (mainly iron and steel), 22 percent for Chile (mainly fertilizer), 11 percent for Brazil (iron and steel), 10 percent for Colombia (cement), two percent for Argentina (iron and steel) and for Mexico (fertilizer), and one percent for Peru (iron and steel) (World Bank, 2023). Byiers and Mednilla (2024) suggest that developing countries have four options to respond: (1) Decarbonize the affected industries; that option may indeed exist for some countries; (2) Emulate the CBAM with a carbon tax of their own. Exporters can deduct carbon prices paid at home from payments under CBAM; yet there is bound to be a considerable difference in carbon prices; (3) Challenge the legality of the CBAM before the WTO, e.g., as a de facto trade barrier; and (4) Divert exports to other countries.

The EU's deforestion regulation (EUDR) aims to reduce the contribution of European consumers to deforestation and biodiversity loss. It bans imports of products from land deforested or degraded after December 31, 2020. It applies to cattle, cocoa, coffee, palm oil, soya, wood, and other products that contain these commodities (Weinhardt & De Ville, 2024) and could affect up to 22 percent of Latin America's exports to the EU (Celiku et al., 2024).

In contrast to the CBAM, where Latin American exporters are likely to be large corporations with a greater capacity to respond, the deforestation legislation will also affect many smaller producers. EUDR requires geolocation data collection down to the plot level and their traceability throughout the upstream supply chain (Celiku et al., 2024). Significant assistance will be needed to put such a system in place so that small and medium-sized producers are able to comply with the requirements.

The CBAM will be phased in gradually during 2026–2034, while the deforestation regulations are scheduled to start in mid-2025 for medium and large companies and mid-2026 for small producers. Both measures are important for the advancement of the green transition in Europe and globally. However, they were conceived without input from and consideration of the capabilities or priorities of developing economies, and they need to be reformed in ways that recognize developing countries' differential capabilities to respond. Tandon and Merle (2024) point out that the EU had an 18-year head start in developing a well-functioning carbon market. Developing countries need resources, time, and technical wherewithal to do the same. Reform efforts should include a transfer of revenues from the CBAM scheme to exporting developing countries to support efforts to decarbonize there, as well as technology transfer and technical assistance (Sasmal, 2024).[9]

Broadening Fiscal Space

The second key factor constraining the implementation of an IGD agenda is the availability of financial resources. Currently, the fiscal space needed is considerably greater than the space available. While spending priorities and needs vary across countries, all will need a big push in domestic resource mobilization as well as more funding from international sources. That, in turn, calls for significant changes in the structure and collection of domestic public revenues and for changes in the global financial architecture.

Needed Versus Actual Fiscal Space

A cost estimate of an inclusive green strategy requires an assessment of the cost of industrial policies, mitigation and adaptation, and social inclusion. At the aggregate level, we have some estimates of the funds needed for a green transition and for specific social goals, both for the Global South broadly and Latin America specifically. But there is little information on the cost of industrial policies given goal and country specificity; DiPippo et al. (2022) mentioned in Chap. 2 is an exception.

[9] The expected annual revenue from the CBAM is €1.5 billion annually (in 2018 prices) as of 2028 (Tandon & Le Merle, 2024).

With respect to the green transition, there is a large gap between the funding needed and the funding that has materialized to date.[10] The cost of moving toward clean energy lies primarily in the large start-up costs, since the actual cost of energy generation is often lower than from new gas or oil plants.[11] And, in a cost benefit analysis, these costs need to be weighed against the savings from importing fossil fuels, the capital goods and material needed for fossil fuel extraction, and the environmental costs of fossil fuel production.[12]

De Miguel et al. (2024) estimate that annual investments in the electric system and infrastructure which LAC countries need to comply with NDC commitments amount to 3.7–4.94 percent of regional GDP between 2023 and 2030 (see Table 3.3).[13] But in 2020, actual climate finance from all sources amounted only to $22.9 billion, 0.48 percent of regional GDP. Of the total, multilateral development banks accounted for 46.6 percent, green bonds for 41 percent, national development banks for 6.7 percent, climate funds for 2.9 percent, and other local resources for 2.8 percent. The most dramatic change in funding sources over the period 2013–2020 was the decline in the share of national development banks (57.6 percent in 2013) and the rise of green bonds (none in 2013).

Considering financing requirements more broadly, Galindo et al. (2022) conclude that annual financial needs for a just green transition in Latin America fall in the range of 7–19 percent of regional GDP by 2030; responding to social challenges would add an additional 5–11 percent of GDP. And Castellani et al. (2019) estimate that addressing infrastructure needs and extreme poverty in LAC requires spending of 10.6 percent of

[10] The Taskforce for Climate, Development, and the IMF (2024) identifies three big gaps: (1) between the commitments countries around the world have made under their NDCs and the commitments needed to meet Paris Agreement goals; (2) between countries' NDC commitments and the CO_2 reductions they have actually achieved; and (3) between funding needed and the funding that materialized.

[11] In 2022, the weighted average cost of electricity from solar PV was $0.049/kWh, and $0.033/kWh for onshore wind, nearly 50 percent cheaper than the cheapest fossil fuel option (IRENA, 2023).

[12] The IMF estimates that, on a global level, the benefits of accelerating the green transition outweigh the costs, and that global output would be 7 percent higher with a transition to net zero by 2050 compared to continuation of current policies (Mehrhoff, 2023).

[13] They do not include data on needed investments in agriculture, cattle ranching, deforestation, and other use of land because they are very difficult to get. The modeling assumes that temperature increases will be kept below 1.5 percent by 2050.

Table 3.3 Annual investment requirements to comply with NDC commitments: Latin America and Caribbean, 2023–2030 (share of GDP)

Sector	*Share of regional GDP*
Total mitigation	*2.30–3.11*
Energy sector	0.22–0.97
Infrastructure: transport	2.0
Electric public transport	0.02–0.08
Total adaptation	*1.40–1.83*
Poverty reduction	0.05–0.46
Infrastructure: irrigation	0.10
Infrastructure: water and sanitation	0.70
Infrastructure: flood control	0.28
Integral early warning system	0.012
Biodiversity (protected areas)	0.26–0.28
Total investment	*3.70–4.94*

regional GDP in 2030, while addressing infant mortality and completion of secondary education would add another 5.4 percent of GDP.

For the Global South as a whole, Bhattacharya et al. (2022) estimate the additional funding needs for human capital, sustainable infrastructure, and adaption and resilience in the Global South (without China) at $3 trillion by 2030: $1.8 trillion for climate action and $1.2 trillion for attaining other SDGs. Added to already existing funding, $3 trillion would bring total funding in 2030 to $5.9 trillion.

The Rio and Paris Agreements recognized the principle of Common, but Differentiated Responsibilities for countries to address climate change, and the need for countries in the Global North to provide financial assistance to developing countries. However, the specification of amounts was left to subsequent negotiations at the Conference of Parties (COP). At COP15 (2009), developed countries committed to supporting the green transition in developing countries with an annual $100 billion by 2020; that goal was met for the first time only in 2022. At COP29 (2024), they increased the annual amount to $300 billion by 2035. COP27 (2022) established and COP28 (2023) operationalized a Loss and Damage Fund to compensate poor countries for losses from adverse climate change impacts. As of early 2025, $741 million had been pledged to the fund. In light of the needs and the urgency for action, all these commitments are highly insufficient.

Filling the large funding gaps for an inclusive green transition will require a considerable increase in domestic resource mobilization and in funding from international sources. In the next section, I focus on how Latin American countries can broaden the fiscal space, and in the subsequent section on needed changes in the international financial architecture to increase funding for developing economies.

National Policies for Increasing Fiscal Space

To start with, it is important to recognize that, over the past 25 years, government revenue as a share of GDP has increased in each of the RR-LAC: on average, from 14.3 percent in 2000/2001 to 19.5 percent in 2021/2022 excluding social security contributions, and from 17.5 percent to 22.2 percent, when they are included.[14] There is considerable variation across countries, with Argentina, Brazil, and Uruguay at the high end and Paraguay and Mexico at the low end (see Table 3.4). Nonetheless, for most countries, tax revenue will need to increase further to support an IGD strategy.

The green transition has positive and negative impacts on fiscal space. On the one hand, the demand for fossil fuels will decrease in the medium run, thus leading to a reduction in export and tax revenues for fossil fuel exporters.[15] Brazil, Bolivia, Colombia, Ecuador, and Mexico will be particularly impacted given their dependence on energy exports (see Table 1.1. again). How much each country will be affected in the end depends on how diversified it is and whether it can keep or gain market share as higher-cost producers drop out (Mesa Puyo et al., 2024). On the other hand, countries with sizeable reserves of critical minerals will see increased demand for these minerals, which can boost public revenues: Argentina, Brazil, Bolivia, Chile, Peru, and Mexico (see Table 1.1). That is the window of opportunity that countries need to take advantage of for embarking on an inclusive green agenda.

[14] There are no data for Venezuela.

[15] Solano-Rodriguez et al. (2019, p. 1) estimate that LAC countries could lose fiscal revenues of $1.3–$1.6 trillion if there is stringent global climate action. With a 50 percent probability of keeping global temperature increases at 1.5 °C by 2050, nearly 60 percent of proven oil and natural gas reserves and 90 percent of coal reserves have to stay in the ground (Mesa Puyo et al., 2024, p. 2).

Table 3.4 Tax structure, non-renewable natural resources, and wealth (2021–2022 average)

	Total tax revenue/ GDP	*Direct tax revenue/ GDP*	*Indirect tax revenue/ GDP*	*Social security contributions/ GDP*	*Property taxes/ GDP*	*Total public revenue from non-renewable resources/GDP*	*Total public revenue from non-renewable natural resources/ total public revenue*	*Total natural resource rents/GDP (2021)*	*Fossil fuel subsidies/ GDP*
(1)	(2)	(3)	(4)	(5)	(6)	(7)	(8)	(9)	(10)
ARG	29.3	8.4	15.6	4.4	2.0	0.7	3.9	2.5	3.1
BOL	23.2	3.3	11.8	5.9	0.3	6.8	24.6	9.0	6.3
BRA	33.0	10.7	14.3	8.0	1.6	3.4	11.9	7.2	0.3
CH	23.2	10.6	11.6	1.1	1.1	3.9	14.9	16.3	0.1
COL	19.1	8.2	7.3	2.0	1.6	3.8	16.8	5.2	1.5
ECU	20.1	5.0	10.1	5.0	0.5	14.2	44.8	6.4	2.6
MEX	17.2	8.4	6.0	2.4	0.3	3.2	16.8	3.5	2.9
PAR	14.3	3.0	7.2	4.1	0.2	0	0	0.1	0.4
PER	18.7	7.7	8.6	1.9	0.4	3.2	15.0	12.6	0
URU	25.9	8.8	10.5	6.4	2.0	0	0	0.0	0

Sources: CEPALSTAT online, World Development Indicators

Note: Tax revenue is for general government and includes social security contributions. Non-renewable resources include extraction from hydrocarbon, commercialization and sale of hydrocarbon, and mining. Fossil fuel subsidies include subsidies for production and consumption.

Policy Actions Linked to the Green Transition

The most important policy action to broaden fiscal space is the capture of a larger share of the natural resource rents. That is one of the big opportunities afforded by the green transition. In the previous chapter we saw that lithium-rich countries have not taken sufficient advantage of the tax revenue-generating possibilities. The same is true for other critical minerals and fossil fuels. Natural resource rents are much higher than the revenue governments currently get from non-renewable natural resources (see columns 7 and 9 in Table 3.4). The gap is particularly large in Brazil, Chile, and Peru.

Appropriating a larger share of the rent is easier when extraction involves direct government participation, as is the case for national oil companies, e.g., in Argentina, Brazil, Colombia, and Mexico, or mining corporations, e.g., Chile's CODELCO, the world's largest state-owned copper producer. It may be harder when companies are owned by multinationals, especially if they are protected by tax stability agreements or the home country has an IIA with the Latin American host country which includes ISDS. An important reason to terminate ISDS.

A reduction in fossil fuel subsidies and a gradual introduction of a carbon tax are two policy measures which have the dual benefit of raising public revenue while shifting production and consumption incentives from fossil fuels to clean energy. The share of fossil fuel subsidies in GDP is significant in Argentina, Bolivia, Colombia, Ecuador, and Mexico, while negligible in the other countries (see Table 3.4); all are below the global average of 7 percent of GDP (Black et al., 2023). Over time, these resources should be redirected to support advances in clean energy, as discussed in Chap. 2.

During the past decade, five Latin American countries implemented a carbon tax: Mexico (2014), Chile (2017), Colombia (2017), Argentina (2018), and Uruguay (2022). Because of the narrow base and low carbon prices, the revenue generated has been very small to date. In 2022, revenues as a share of GDP amounted to 0.01 percent in Mexico, 0.03 percent in Argentina and Colombia, 0.06 percent in Chile, and 0.36 percent in Uruguay (De Miguel et al., 2024, p. 59). Colombia is the only country where the carbon tax revenue is used specifically to address environmental goals. Based on a simulation with a net zero emissions goal for hydrocarbon exporters by 2050, Titelman et al. (2022) conclude that a steadily increasing carbon tax would cover the revenue losses from hydrocarbon only in Brazil and Colombia, but not in Bolivia, Ecuador, and Mexico.[16]

Last but definitely not least, there is significant growth potential for green, social, sustainability, and sustainability-linked (GSSS) bonds, which have increased considerably over the past few years. In 2023, GSSS bonds made up 50 percent of total sovereign bond issues compared to 36 percent in 2022 (OECD, 2024, p. 8). Uruguay's 2022 sustainability-linked bonds are particularly interesting as they are structured to include not only rewards, but also penalties (IEA, 2023).[17] If countries have to renegotiate international debt, they should consider debt swap instruments, e.g., debt for climate or nature swaps, blue bonds, green bonds, and sustainability-linked bonds (Alayza et al., 2023).

Policy Actions Addressing Structural Issues

A different set of policies needs to address the structural issues behind the relatively low tax intake in most countries: the lack of progressivity in the tax structure, profit-shifting and tax evasion, and the narrow tax base.

One way to make the tax structure more progressive is to tax wealth at a higher rate. According to the World Bank (2024, p. 4), 80 percent of wealth in LAC is in real estate, including in the top 10 percent of earners. But the public revenue share from property taxes is low (see Table 3.4). The World Bank study suggests that the problem is not low tax rates, but dramatic undervaluation of properties. However, a significant percentage of wealth is held abroad. For 2021, the estimates range from one percent in Brazil to nearly 14 percent in Uruguay (Tax Justice Network, 2024).

Another important measure for increasing tax revenue it to rein in profit shifting and tax evasion and avoidance. ECLAC (2024, p. 14) estimates that tax non-compliance in LAC was $433 billion in 2023. Tax non-compliance from income and profits was 6.7 percent of GDP, nearly as high as the 7.2 percent of the tax actually collected. Value added tax avoidance was 2.1 percent of GDP compared to the actual receipt of 7.3 percent. While some countries have adopted measures to reduce evasion, much remains to be done.

[16] They assume that the carbon tax would reach $55/ton in Bolivia and Ecuador, and $451/ton in Colombia, Brazil, and Mexico.

[17] If the government exceeds its sustainability goals by 2025, it pays a lower interest rate; and if it fails to do so, it pays a higher rate. The specific sustainability goals were a reduction in GHG emissions per unit of GDP and preservation of native forests (IEA, 2023, p. 37).

It is clear that the problem of tax evasion cannot be solved at the national level alone and needs international cooperation. Existing international structures are conducive to tax evasion and avoidance, including undervaluation and overvaluation of exports and imports, services transactions and royalties, and tax evasion structures that take advantage of preferential regimes and double taxation treaties. International tax cooperation could prevent profit shifting and tax erosion and raise hundreds of millions of dollars annually (Zucman, 2024). In late 2021, the Organization for Economic Co-operation and Development (OECD) adopted the Base Erosion and Profit Shifting Agreement. While a step in the right direction, it has been criticized widely for being insufficient (Pillar 1 only targets the richest multinationals), and for the minimal corporation tax rate of 15 percent (Pillar 2) being too low (Stiglitz, 2023). In November 2024, the UN General Assembly voted to begin negotiations on a new framework convention on international tax cooperation, giving greater voice to countries in the Global South.

The establishment of the Regional Platform for Tax Cooperation in Latin America and the Caribbean (PTLAC for the acronym in Spanish) in July 2023 is a significant step toward regional cooperation on tax matters. It provides a forum for finance ministers of the region to discuss shared tax challenges and come together on key issues (taxes for climate change, greater tax progressivity, taxes for digital services).[18]

Given the large size of the informal sector in many Latin American countries, it is critical that the tax base is expanded. As highlighted in Chap. 2, that will require concerted efforts to support SMEs to create more employment.

Political Challenges

While there are several ways to increase public revenue, the main challenge to implementation is political: Which interest coalitions can be assembled in support of any of the measures discussed above? Ondetti (2023) suggests that the extent to which a leftist government has challenged private property is a key element for understanding differences in tax ratios among Latin American countries. He argues that radical threats to property, especially in agriculture, led to a more united business sector and increased persistence of lower (or at least not increased) tax ratios under a subsequent

[18] For first tangible gains of PTLAC for 2024 see OECD (2025).

right-leaning government. Thus, he concludes that incremental redistribution, rather than radical change, has a greater chance to succeed.

The tax reforms of the Petro Administration in Colombia offer a good example of the conditions that allow tax reforms to work. Petro assumed the presidency on August 7, 2022; he introduced a tax reform to Congress on August 8, and after negotiations and adjustments, a reform was passed on December 13, 2022. The main elements were greater progressivity in income taxes (reduction of taxes on low-income households, increase in wealth tax, elimination of a number of exemptions) and measures toward a green transition (surtax on income of oil and coal companies, carbon tax on coal, tax on sugar and sodium-rich highly processed foods, tax on single-use plastic for packing (PwC, 2022)). The reform did not include an increase in the value added tax, a lesson learned from the reform of the prior Duque government, which had led to massive protests and failed.

When asked about lessons from the Colombian tax reform for other countries in Latin America, then minister of finance José Antonio Ocampo highlighted two key factors which made the Colombian reform successful: a political coalition and a willingness to negotiate.[19] First, the Petro government was backed by a political coalition, an alliance of representatives of parties and political movements from the left and center-left ("Pacto Historico"), which had a majority in Congress.[20] Second, the government was willing to negotiate with key constituencies and settle for what was possible and not hold out for everything hoped for.

When the Petro government submitted a second tax reform in late 2024, it did not pass, as the coalition had broken apart over healthcare reform, and corruption scandals had undermined the legitimacy of the government.

Needed Reforms of the Global Financial Architecture

International financial inflows have to complement domestic efforts to increase the needed funding for an inclusive green strategy. The current global financial architecture has not met expectations and needs. Key factors behind insufficient public financial flows from the Global North to the Global South are the voluntary nature of industrialized countries'

[19] Author interview, November 21, 2023.

[20] That coalition broke apart in early 2023 over healthcare reform, and "Pacto Historico" lost by a considerable margin in local and regional elections in late October 2023.

commitments and the current rules governing multilateral development banks (MDBs).

Where is the additional annual $3 trillion supposed to come from that Bhattacharya et al. (2022) estimate is needed by 2030? The G20 Independent Expert Group (2023) offers a concrete proposal for funding targets by source: two-thirds of the $3 trillion should come from domestic sources and one-third from external funding. Of the $1 billion in external funding, $500 billion from private capital and $500 billion from official development assistance (ODA), with $180 billion concessional finance and the rest non-concessional funding. Of the $500 billion of ODA, $260 billion from MDBs, and the rest from bilaterals and other multilaterals.

As desirable as it would be for the private sector to provide half the needed external funding, there are good reasons to be skeptical. While there are a number of proposals for de-risking private investments and increasing public–private financing collaborations (G20 Independent Expert Group, 2023; Bridgetown Initiative, n.d.), the reality is that private investors mainly invest where it is most profitable and where the largest incentives are offered. They will shy away from long-term investments (Lebdioui, 2024). Thus, invoking large-scale private participation is often a fig leaf to cover the greatly insufficient public funding, e.g., the vague promise at COP29 to raise $1.3 trillion by 2035, mainly from private sources.

And if private investors don't step up, public providers will have to furnish the bulk of external funding. To that end, there have been a number of proposals for reforming the Global Financial Architecture. For the World Bank and the IMF, proposals focus on increased funding (including a new allocation of special drawing rights (SDRs) and a reassignment to developing countries of the SDRs developed countries do not use), inclusion of structural transformation and green transition needs in fiscal responsibility and debt relief, and more voice and participation of developing countries (Bhattacharya et al., 2022; G20 Independent Expert Group, 2023; Taskforce on Climate, Development, and the IMF, 2024; Zucker-Marques et al., 2024).

The G20 Independent Expert Group also calls on MDBs to reconsider their lending to upper middle-income countries, which is particularly relevant for Latin American countries. For example, the World Bank should lend to upper middle-income countries which have exceeded the Graduation Discussion Income Threshold, since they are most likely to undertake climate action.

In recent years, China has become an increasingly important source of climate-related funding, globally and in LAC countries. Over the period 2013–2022, China provided and mobilized an estimated $44.9 billion in climate-related finance for developing countries (Liu et al., 2024): 38 percent were channeled through bilateral public finance, 34 percent through multilateral finance, and 26 percent through export credits (see also Chap. 5). With respect to Latin America though, China's development lending (not just for climate) has declined in recent years. Between 2019 and 2023, China Development Bank (CDB) and the Export-Import Bank of China lent, on average, $1.3 billion annually to LAC, down from $25 billion just from the CDB in 2010 (Myers & Ray, 2024).

Besides bilateral and multilateral sources, there are other possibilities to mobilize international resources in support of climate mitigation, adaptation, and loss and damage in the Global South. They include a global financial transaction tax, redirecting the revenue from the EU's CBAM to investments in developing economies, a tax on maritime shipping, and a tax on air travel.

For their part, developing countries in Latin America and elsewhere need clear plans and strategies that provide direction and specify projects in need of funding. Ideally, they establish country platforms which make the projects legible and transparent. That would make it easier for potential bilateral and multilateral lenders to target funding and to coordinate among themselves.

Final Considerations

The discussion in this chapter has shown the need and possibilities for reforms at the national and international level to increase policy and fiscal space for the implementation of an IDG strategy. Reforms at the international level take a long time, and the chances for success have become significantly more uncertain and volatile with the willful policymaking of the second Trump Administration.

That puts the focus for reform policies primarily on the national and regional level. The cost of bilateral trade and investment treaties has been a dramatic reduction in policy space. Thus, governments would do well to reassess the value of these treaties as they currently stand. Procurement in particular is a powerful tool for creating a market for new products by domestic producers.

There is power in numbers and in speaking with one voice, whether that is on tax matters in international fora, e.g., as a result of deliberations in PTLAC, or on the cancellation of bilateral investment treaties with ISDS. We have to stop thinking of regional initiatives as comprising all of Latin or South America, as governments have very different agendas and outlooks, e.g., Milei in Argentina and Sheinbaum in Mexico. It may be more feasible to form a coalition of progressive governments who agree on joint actions and demands in pushing for aspects of an inclusive green development agenda. Such a coalition is likely to face pressure from Washington's hypersensitivity to anything that might strengthen the strategic autonomy of the countries in the region. But coordinated action will increase the likelihood of success.

References

Abugattas, L., & Paus, E. (2008). Policy space for a capability-centered development strategy for Latin America. In D. Sanchez-Ancochea & K. Shadlen (Eds.), *The political economy of hemispheric integration. Responding to globalization in the Americas* (pp. 113–143). Palgrave Macmillan.

Agosin, M. (2023). Productive development policy for Chile: An alternative to stagnation. *CEPAL Review, 139*, 117–133.

Aisbett, E., et al. (2018). *Rethinking international investment governance: Principles for the 21st century.* Columbia Center for Sustainable Development.

Alayza, N., Laxton, V., & Neuneubel, C. (2023). *Developing countries won't beat the climate crisis without tackling rising debt.* World Resources Institute. https://www.wri.org/insights/debt-climate-action-developing-countries

Bhattacharya, A., et al. (2022). *Financing a big investment push in emerging markets and developing economies for sustainable, resilient and inclusive recovery and growth.* Grantham Research Institute on Climate Change and the Environment, London School of Economics and Political Science, and Washington, DC: Brookings Institution.

Black, S., Parry, I., & Vernon-Lin, N. (2023). *Fossil fuel subsidies surged to record $ 7 trillion.* https://www.imf.org/en/Blogs/Articles/2023/08/24/fossil-fuel-subsidies-surged-to-record-7-trillion

Brada, J., Drabek, Z., & Iwasaki, I. (2021). Does investor protection increase foreign direct investment? A meta-analysis. *Journal of Economic Surveys, 35*(1), 34–70. https://doi.org/10.1111/joes.12392

Bridgetown Initiative. (n.d.) *Bridgetown initiative on the reform of the international development and climate finance architecture.* https://www.bridgetown-initiative.org/bridgetown-initiative-3-0/

Byiers, B., & Mednilla, A. (2024). *The EU's carbon border adjustment mechanism and developing countries: Threats, opportunities and strategic responses.* ECDPM. Discussion paper no. 380.

Castellani, F., Olarreaga, M., Panizza, U., & Zhou, Y. (2019). *Investment gaps in Latin America and the Caribbean.* International Development Policy. https://doi.org/10.4000/poldev.2894

Celiku, B., et al. (2024, July 31) *The impact of European Union deforestation regulation: Four lessons from Peru's journey.* World Bank Blog.

Chang, H.-J. (2002). *Kicking away the ladder. Development strategy in historical perspective.* Anthem Press.

De Miguel, C., et al. (2024) *Necesidades de financiamiento y objetivos climáticos en América Latina y el Caribe.* CEPAL, Documentos de Proyectos (LC/TS. 2024.47).

DiPippo, G., Mazzocco, I., & Kennedy, S. (2022). *Red ink. Estimating industrial policy spending in comparative perspective.* Center for Strategic and International Studies.

Du, M. (2023). Explaining China's approach to investor-state dispute settlement reform: A contextual perspective. *European Law Journal, 28*(4–6), 281–303. https://doi.org/10.1111/eulj.12468

Duarte, N., & Rangel, D. (2023). New directions in international investment law: Alternatives for improvement. In *CAROLA Policy Brief.* Center for the Advancement of the Rule of Law in the Americas, Georgetown University.

ECLAC. (2024). *Fiscal panorama of Latin America and the Caribbean 2024.* Fiscal policy for addressing the challenges of climate change. Economic Commission on Latin America and the Caribbean.

Galindo, L. M., Hoffman, B., & Vogt-Schilb, A. (2022). *How much will it cost to achieve climate goals in Latin America and the Caribbean?* (Inter-American development bank working paper IDB-WP-01310).

Goerg, H., & Greenaway, D. (2004) Much ado about nothing? Do domestic firms really benefit from foreign direct investment?. *The World Bank Observer*, *19*(2), 171–197.

Greenfield, P., & Weston, P. (2025, March 5). Revealed: How Wall Street is making millions betting against green laws. *The Guardian.* https://www.theguardian.com/environment/2025/mar/05/revealed-how-wall-street-is-making-millions-betting-against-green-laws-isds-aoe

Hopewell, K. (2024). The surprise return of development policy space in the multilateral trading system: What the WTO appellate body blockage means for the developmental state. *Review of International Political Economy, 31*(4), 1245–1270. https://doi.org/10.1080/09692290.2024.2303681

G20 Independent Expert Group. (2023). Strengthening multilateral development banks. *The triple agenda.* https://www.gihub.org/resources/publications/strengthening-multilateral-development-banks-the-triple-agenda-report-of-the-g20-independent-experts-group/

International Energy Agency (IEA). (2023). *Latin America energy outlook.* www.iea.org

IRENA (International Renewable Energy Agency). (2023). *Renewables competitiveness accelerates, despite cost inflation.* https://www.irena.org/News/pressreleases/2023/Aug/Renewables-Competitiveness-Accelerates-Despite-Cost-inflation#:~:text=Between%202010%20and%202022%2C%20solar,the%20cheapest%20fossil%20fuel%20globally

Lebdioui, A. (2024). *Survival of the greenest. Economic transformation in a climate-conscious world.* UNU WIDER and Cambridge University Press. https://doi.org/10.1017/9781009339414

Liu, S., Wang Y., Ma Z., Zou, C. Q., & Zhou L. (2024). *China's international climate-related finance provision and mobilization for South-South cooperation* (Working paper). World Resources Institute. https://doi.org/10.46830/wriwp.24.00036

Mehranvar, L., et al. (2024). *Breaking free: Strategies for governments on terminating investment treaties and removing ISDS provisions.* Columbia Center on Sustainable Development.

Mehrhoff, J. (2023). Benefits of accelerating the climate costs outweigh the costs. *IMF Blog.* https://www.imf.org/en/Blogs/Articles/2023/12/05/benefits-of-accelerating-the-climate-transition-outweigh-the-costs

Mesa Puyo, D., et al. (2024) *Key challenges faced by fossil fuel exporters during the energy transition.* IMF Staff Climate Note 2024/001.

Müller, B., & Ghiotto, L. (2024). *Impacts of investment arbitration against Latin America and the Caribbean.* Transnational Institute.

Myers, M., & Ray, R. (2024). *Feeling the stones. Chinese development finance to Latin America and the Caribbean, 2023.* Global Development Policy Center, Boston University.

OECD. (2024). *The surge of green, social, sustainability and sustainability-linked (GSSS) bonds in Latin America and the Caribbean* (OECD development policy papers no. 56).

OECD. (2025). *Global forum on transparency and exchange of information for tax purposes. Tax transparency in Latin America 2025.* OECD.

Ondetti, G. (2023). Redistributive threats, development models, and taxation in Latin America. In P. Fehling & H.-J. Burchardt (Eds.), *Taxation and inequality. New perspectives on political economy and tax regimes* (pp. 157–175). Routledge.

Paus, E. (2005). *Foreign investment, development, and globalization. Can Costa Rica become Ireland?* Palgrave Macmillan.

Public Citizen. (2024). *The worst of the worst. Egregious corporate attacks on public interest policies.* https://gtwaction.org/egregious-isds-cases/

Public Citizen Global Trade Watch. (2018). *Termination of bilateral investment treaties has not negatively affected countries' foreign direct investment inflows.* Public Citizen Research Brief. https://www.citizen.org/wp-content/uploads/pcgtw_fdi-inflows-from-bit-termination_1.pdf

PwC (Price Waterhouse Cooper). (2022, January 1). *Colombia passes major tax reform effective.* https://www.pwc.com/us/en/services/tax/library/colombia-passes-major-tax-reform-effective-january-1.html#:~:text=The%20new%20law%20becomes%20effective,local%20operations%20and%20financing%20strategies.&text=The%20Tax%20Reform%20Law%3A,general%20CIT%20rate%20at%2035%25

Rangel, D., et al. (2023). *Turning the tide: How to harness the Americas partnership for economic prosperity to deliver an ISDS-free Americas.* Columbia Center on Sustainable Development.

Reiter, L., & Bellak, C. (2020). Effects of BITs on FDI: The role of publication bias. In J. Chaisse, L. Choukroune, & S. Jusoh (Eds.), *Handbook of international investment law and policy.* Springer. https://doi.org/10.1007/978-981-13-5744-2_123-1

Sasmal, S. (2024). *New approaches and challenges regarding trade, climate action, and the WTO.* Columbia Center of Sustainable Investment.

Shadlen, K. (2006). Exchanging development for market access? Deep integration and industrial policy under multilateral and regional-bilateral trade agreements. *Review of International Political Economy, 12*(5), 750–775. https://doi.org/10.1080/09692290500339685

Solano-Rodríguez, B., et al. (2019). *Implications for climate change targets on oil production and fiscal revenues in Latina America and the Caribbean.* Interamerican Development Bank.

Stiglitz, J. (2023). Discurso pronunciado en la Primera Cumbre de Latinoamérica y el Caribe para una tributación global incluyente, sostenible y equitativa. In FEDESARROLLO (Ed.), *Desafíos de la tributación global: Hacía una tributación global incluyente, sostenible y equitativa para América Latina y el Caribe* (pp. 21–30). FEDESARROLLO.

Tandon, S., & Le Merle, K. (2024). Evaluating the impact of CBAM on developing countries. In *The EU's new approach to multilateralism and trade.* Foundation for European Progressive Studies & National Institute of Public Finance and Policy.

Taskforce on Climate, Development, and the IMF. (2024). *A Transformative action agenda for achieving climate and development goals.* Global Development Policy Center, Boston University.

Tax Justice Network. (2024). *State of tax justice 2024.* https://taxjustice.net/reports/the-state-of-tax-justice-2024/

Thrasher, R. (2017). *Policy space for jobs and clean energy. Trade, investment rules and local content requirements in renewable energy policies* (CEGI working paper 012). Global Development Policy Center, Boston University.

Thrasher, R. (2021). *Constraining development: How global trade rules conflict with national development goals.* Anthem Press.

Titelman, D., et al. (2022). *Fiscal impact estimates of a net-zero emissions transition for major hydrocarbon producers in Latin America and the Caribbean.* Taskforce on Climate, Development, and the IMF. https://www.bu.edu/gdp/files/2022/04/TF-WP-004-EN-FIN.pdf

Weinhardt, C., & De Ville, F. (2024). The geoeconomic turn in EU trade and investment policy: Implications for developing countries. *Politics and Governance., 12.* https://doi.org/10.17645/pag.8217

World Bank. (2023). *Relative CBAM exposure index.* https://www.worldbank.org/en/data/interactive/2023/06/15/relative-cbam-exposure-index#2

World Bank. (2024). *Taxing wealth for equity and growth.* World Bank.

Zucker-Marques, M., Gallagher, K. P., Volz, U., et al. (2024). *Defaulting on development and climate. Debt sustainability and the race for the 2030 agenda and Paris Agreement.* Boston University Global Development Center, Centre for Sustainable Finance; SOAS, University of London; Heinrich Böll Foundation.

Zucman, G. 2024. *A blueprint for a coordinated minimum effective taxations standard for ultra-high-net-worth individuals.* https://www.taxobservatory.eu//www-site/uploads/2024/06/report-g20.pdf

CHAPTER 4

Building National Power Blocs to Drive an Inclusive Green Transition

Rafael Domínguez

Abstract This chapter explores the conditions necessary to build development-oriented coalitions that support an inclusive green transition in Latin American countries, moving away from extractivism by utilizing natural resource wealth. The strategy of leveraging natural resources to diversify the economy impacts state–society relations, requiring an analysis of values, interests, and historical context, across the dividing lines of vertical and horizontal inequalities. Despite structural constraints, there is potential for progressive agency behind dependent development. Factors such as social stratification, rising expectations, demographic structure, and concerns about inequalities suggest potential electoral support for green transformation. However, challenges arise due to political dynamics, changing social preferences, and internal polarization. The chapter argues that transformative political leadership supported by development-oriented coalitions is crucial for overcoming the middle-income trap and achieving the inclusive green transition, with an active role of the state as environmental agency.

Keywords Soft state • Social movements • Elites • Polarization • Extractivism • Extractive bargains • Informality • Transformative leadership • Green developmental state

E. Paus, R. Domínguez, *Toward Inclusive Development in Latin America*, Palgrave Studies in Latin American Heterodox Economics, https://doi.org/10.1007/978-3-032-08588-7_4

"We do not try to place theoretical limits on the probable course of future events. This will depend… on collective action guided by political wills that make work what is structurally barely possible."
—Fernando Henrique Cardoso and Enzo Faletto (1979)

This chapter discusses the conditions of possibility for building development-oriented coalitions that promote an inclusive green transition to break away from extractivism by leveraging the very wealth of natural resources. This has been a hotly debated topic in LAC for decades within the framework of the dependency research program of political economy. The strategy of utilizing natural resources to diversify the economy and reduce dependency impacts state–society relations, requiring consideration of actors' values, interests, and preferences in a structural and historical context-specific analysis. I argue that there is open space for a progressive agency behind dependent development despite internal and external structural constraints.

Social stratification, rising expectations, demographic structure, and strong concern about interpersonal and intergenerational inequalities are key factors which suggest a priori potential electoral support for an agenda of inclusive and green structural transformation. However, several issues arise in state–society relations, political dynamics, and changing social preferences, which make that support more fragile than expected. Therefore, the progressive governments of the second Pink Tide face major challenges in a context dominated internally by the new role of social movements and their impact on political (ideological) and affective (emotional) polarization controlled by elites with veto power and strong international connections. Meanwhile, on the entangled and volatile international chessboard of energy geopolitics and fragmentation of geo-economic spheres, greater external vulnerability (unequal trade and ecological exchange) and financial and technological dependence affect economic growth and structural change while catalyzing distributive conflicts.

I highlight the critical importance of transformative political leadership to build and manage social coalitions based not only on strengthening the state with enhanced fiscal, regulatory, administrative, and planning capacities, but also on embedded autonomy to drive the inclusive green development (IGD) transition. As the long-term development agenda must be inclusive at the national level and just within international politics, it cannot be left to the market and democratic political calculus of short-termism. Latin American countries need to bring the state back in, as a new normative ideal (green state), and operational apparatus (environmental-developmental state) with enhanced capabilities for implementing a new generation of industrial policies (see Chap. 2). Such a reformist agenda must go beyond ECLAC's timid productive development policies. It must fully engage in long-term institutional and economic change to escape the middle-income trap.

Missing Actors for Another Development in Latin America

Who are the actors and constellations of interests that can drive the transition toward IGD in Latin America? This question is addressed in the following sections through an analysis of state–society relations and the analysis of different actors under neoliberal policy regimes. It updates reflections by Fernando Henrique Cardoso regarding the failure of state-led development under import-substituting industrialization to share the fruits of technological progress at high environmental costs (Cardoso, 1977). The Brazilian sociologist pointed out the Achilles heel of alternative development: the lack of "historical subjects of transformations" (Cardoso, 1980, p. 858). Another development related to emerging social movements—then, political minorities like "feminism, anti-racial struggles, youth movements, urban protest organizations, forums for habitat and the environment" (Cardoso, 1977, p. 33)—suffered equally from the problem of lacking the historical agent beyond the international bureaucracies (Cardoso, 1980).

Today, unlike then, the socio-ecological transformation advocated by ECLAC's ecological neo-structuralism does indeed have a group of potential actors promoting and supporting this new kind of other development, in the context of environmental mobilization (Rossi, 2023) and reactivation of state capitalism under the umbrella of a developmental-environmental or green entrepreneurial state to drive decarbonization (Kastelli et al., 2023; Allan, 2024; Larsen, 2024). There is no doubt that the success of the IDG transition driven by progressive governments will depend on empowering popular sectors while undermining the political capacity of traditional economic elites (Chiasson-LeBel & Larrabure, 2019). In addition, the emergence of a green state will also depend on broad agreements with the new or reconverted elites favoring or enabling a green transition (Bull, 2022).

Several authors in ECLAC's intellectual ecosystem have recently reflected on Cardoso's historical agent problem highlighting the importance of development-oriented coalitions (Rubio, 2023; Porcile, 2024; Domínguez, 2024; Oreiro, 2024). And ECLAC (2024a, p. 52) itself talks of the political economy of "stakeholder coalitions (technical, bureaucratic social, academic, business or political actors)" promoting socio-ecological transition.

This return to political economy requires delineating the subject of transformation, for which Cardoso and his co-author Enzo Faletto established the method of historical-structural analysis employed in this chapter. This "comprehensive analysis" (systemic in our wording) examines the specific country conditions in terms of "the way internal and external *structural components* are linked" (Cardoso & Faletto, 1978, pp. 11, 19; emphasis mine), as well as in terms of *agency*: "…the conflict between groups and classes, as well as the social movements that «drive» developing societies" (Cardoso & Faletto, 1978, pp. 17–18). With an empirical and normative-reformist political economy approach, historical-structural analysis merges structure, which influences social stratification, with history analyzing the action of social forces (those that tend to maintain the status quo and those in favor of social change) as well as their respective ideologies. To achieve a successful dependent development strategy (GDP per capita growth driven by industrialization broadly understood) the key factor is pragmatic leadership for transformation leveraging and catalyzing social mobilization (Cardoso & Faletto, 1979).

While Cardoso and Faletto's essay represents the overlooked theoretical source of new developmentalism (Antunes de Oliveira, 2022), the concept of dependent development and the historical-structural analysis of the dependency research program must be updated to the new institutional context of time-space compressed development arising in the 1990s (Whitaker et al., 2020). Today, dependent development needs to resolve the problems of equity and well-being of the majority that were absent in Cardoso and Faletto's concept, in which industrialization enhances income concentration and produces "structural heterogeneity" (Cardoso & Faletto, 1979, p. xxii). Also, the actualization of dependent development must take into account the sustainability dimension (Naseemullah, 2022; Fritz et al., 2022).

After four decades of neoliberal policies, historical-structural analysis also has to include two new issues. First, the effects of the policy regime on the coherence and relationships among the main collective actors in national development (the state, the private sector, workers, and transnational corporations). Second, changes in the international context—institutionalization of international trade and investment agreements with and after the creation of the World Trade Organization in 1995, the China factor (with its accession to the WTO in 2001), and the emission reduction commitments of the Paris Agreement on Climate Change (2015)—have narrowed the policy space available for industrial policies of developmental states (see Chap. 3).

In the context of Latin American countries' compressed development, the China factor weighs heavily (Paus, 2020). China's demand during the past commodity boom exacerbated the reduction of productive complexity and the re-primarization processes brought about by the Washington Consensus. However, the relationship with China also opened the possibility for reversing neoliberal policies in the region, a potential that has not been fully exploited. Given the difficulties in establishing an autonomous LAC regional bloc (Bernal-Meza, 2020), such lost opportunity was due to the preference for bilateral relations with the Asian giant by the private and/or public national elites as junior partners of outward foreign direct investment from China (Wainer, 2023; Bull & Rosales, 2024). In any case, now that China has shifted toward developmental environmentalism, it is necessary to reformulate the question of leadership capable of driving the IGD transition in terms of forging a long-term consensus on institutional reforms among the members of a coalition of the willing (Thurbon et al., 2023).

Historical evidence shows that the developmental state has been the primary driver of development for old and contemporary latecomers (Bresser-Pereira, 2019; Naseemullah, 2023). Thus, to make the seemingly impossible in Latin American countries feasible requires competent, strong, and stable political leadership with a developmental-environmental mindset, along with the capacity of the state apparatus to translate ambitions into action through public policies that ensure effective and equitable solutions. As an internally heterogeneous actor, with different branches that have their own interests and influence, and agents that operate with relative autonomy (Bowles & Andrews, 2023), the state must regain its strategic functions. Certainly, the state's power, resources, and autonomy have been drastically diminished in recent years in favor of capital, which is increasingly connected to transnational capitalism through the finance, insurance, and real estate sectors (Rossi, 2023; Naseemullah, 2023). However, the state must restrain the imbalances between capital and labor as well as capital and the state itself, taking advantage of the green transition agenda, by leveraging internal support for development-oriented coalitions and South-South cooperation and engaging in a foreign policy of active non-alignment (see Chap. 5).

The primary capital-labor contradiction has been overlaid with the fragmented and divisive demands of social movements focused on particular or sectoral causes (Al-Suwaidan & Mazaheri, 2023; Naseemullah, 2023). This changes the social content of "upgrading coalitions" (Doner & Schneider, 2016, p. 611), i.e., the "developmental class coalition" of entrepreneurs, workers, and public bureaucracy to support the developmental state, against the "neoliberal coalition" integrated by landowners, patrimonial capitalists, financiers, the top executive of corporations, the middle-class rentiers, and foreign interests (Bresser-Pereira, 2017, p. 692). Such a development-oriented coalition needs to be greened including the defenders of an environmental agenda of sustainable developmentalism (Albertone, 2025), an interclass constellation of very heterogeneous organizations. They comprise a broad sector of urban middle-class consumers (with students and the feminist movement at the forefront) and even sectors of the financial market exploring opportunities with the energy transition, as well as popular movements of peasants, indigenous people, and women, without forgetting rural and urban informal workers (Alcañiz & Gutiérrez, 2022; Pucheta et al., 2023; Christel & Gutiérrez, 2023; Oreiro, 2024).

Additionally, we need a broadened understanding of embedded autonomy (Clark & Rosales, 2023; Naseemullah, 2023) including both those at the bottom and those at the top. At the bottom, Peter Evans (2010), the other major Brazilian advocate of dependent development alongside Cardoso, proposed an update of the developmentalist state based on creative experimentation and the construction of a more encompassing form of embeddedness beyond the entrepreneurial elite. It is a broader cross-section of society full of conflicting particular interests with whom the twenty-first-century developmental state needs to *politically* negotiate a development strategy. Such a strategy must be based on expanded capabilities (public investment in health, education, and infrastructure), shared returns (transforming discouraged and unqualified potential workers into productive members of the formal labor force), and a lighter ecological footprint. Otherwise, the technocratic capacity of the developmental state will be "sterile and ineffective" (Evans & Heller, 2015, p. 709). At the top, Bull and Aguilar-Støen (2015) analyze the emergence of new elite groups with an environmental background and elite reorientation toward the agenda of inclusive green transformation. In the next two sections, I discuss the implications of bottom and top approaches.

State–Society Relations: What Kind of State, Capacities, and Relations

The current problem of Latin American states is described by ECLAC (2024b, p. 70) as "the trap of low institutional capacity and ineffective governance." This trap is interconnected with two others: the trap of low capacity for growth, via the connections between dysfunctional institutions, higher transaction costs, and increased uncertainty; and the trap of high inequality and low social mobility and cohesion, via the relationships between social exclusion and mistrust in the main institutions of state and democracy. In this section, I analyze these traps in the theoretical-conceptual framework of the soft state, which reaffirms the need for a developmental state in Latin America for the IGD transition.

The low institutional capacity and ineffective governance of Latin American states is reflected in the State Capacity Index.[1] This index uses 21 indicators to measure the extractive capacity to generate revenue, the coercive capacity to enforce the law, and the administrative capacities to delivery public services. The scale ranges from +5 (maximum capacity) to −5 (no capacity). The results allow for a tripartite classification of countries, with Uruguay, Chile, and Argentina with the highest scores; Venezuela, Bolivia, and Paraguay with the lowest; and a heterogeneous group of remaining countries in between (Table 4.1).

A dominant feature in Latin American countries is the distrust in the main institutions of state and democracy, an institutional weakness linked to the level of inequality. Based on their levels of distrust in the branches of state power (executive, legislative, and judicial) and political parties as key democratic institutions, we can distinguish three groups. The first group comprises Uruguay (with the lowest levels of distrust among the 11

[1] https://colinworeilly.com/state-capacity-index/

Table 4.1 State Capacity Index and distrust in institutions (share of people with "little" and "no trust")

Country	*Year*	*State Capacity Index*[a]	*Distrust in institutions*[b]			
			Government	*Congress*	*Judiciary*	*Political parties*
Argentina	2002	1.26	92.2	89.6	90.4	94.4
	2021/23	1.41	76.6	72.8	73.7	81.2
Bolivia	2002	−0.57	81.7	78.3	74.5	86.4
	2021/23	−0.34	70.2	67.9	**76.4**	84.5
Brazil	2002	1.02	74.2	69.9	63.9	84.5
	2021/23	**0.31**	65.6	66.7	60.7	**90.5**
Chile	2002	2.43	55.0	66.6	73.7	84.5
	2021/23	**1.65**	**63.8**	**81.7**	72.5	80.1
Colombia	2002	−0.13	83.3	80.3	71.7	86.1
	2021/23	0.22	72.1	80.3	**73.5**	**88.3**
Ecuador	2002	−0.24	85.8	90.8	84.7	90.1
	2021/23	0.52	**87.0**	85.9	73.5	88.6
Mexico	2002	0.20	80.5	75.1	81.2	85.9
	2021/23	−0.19	61.5	63.1	**84.9**	74.8
Paraguay	2002	−1.61	92.8	84.3	88.1	92.4
	2021/23	−1.02	82.7	77.0	73.5	82.7
Peru[a]	2002	0.58	74.1	73.9	78.5	82.2
	2021/23	**0.50**	**90.2**	**94.5**	**84.9**	**91.9**
Uruguay	2002	2.88	65.9	56.5	52.6	70.1
	2021/23	**2.61**	50.2	46.8	64.3	66.8
Venezuela	2002	−1.36	59.7	61.1	67.1	77.2
	2021/25	**−2.87**	**79.5**	**75.1**	**76.3**	**83.0**

Source: State Capacity Index, https://worldmap.qog.gu.se/; Latinobarómetro Online Analysis

Boldface indicates a worsening of the variable

[a]Data for 2002 (Peru 2005) and 2021

[b]Data for 2023

countries in nearly all categories), Mexico (with the second-lowest levels of distrust in the executive and legislative branches and political parties, although it shares the lowest level of confidence in the judicial branch), and Brazil (with the lowest level of distrust in the judiciary branch). At the opposite end is Peru, with widespread deterioration and the worst levels of distrust in all categories, followed by Ecuador, second-worst in distrust in the executive and legislative branches and third-worst regarding political parties. Between these two extremes lies an amorphous group of countries, with significant variation in individual indicators. These groupings, in comparison with those resulting from the State Capacity Index, suggest that there is no straight connection (with the exception of Uruguay) between lack of state capacity and distrust in institutions.

In Weberian terms, the great majority of Latin American states correspond to the semi-patrimonial variety of poor-quality, unequal, yet durable democracies. They have become veritable engines of discontent, given the high level of dissatisfaction with democracy, neutrality of government, and trust in the police (Table 4.2). In semi-patrimonial states, the rule of law, law enforcement, and equality before the law are for the ruling few. That has a negative impact on the prospects for constructing a high-quality or consolidated democracy: directly, because of the arbitrary use of power by the rulers, and, indirectly, because it hinders the provision of public goods and public services, a necessary condition for the institutionalization of representative political parties (López, 2020; Munck, 2024; Corporación Latinobarómetro, 2024). As highlighted in the latest Latinobarómetro report, "...political parties are exhausted, the parliament is worn out as an institution, the judicial system is delegitimized, and the elites are discredited" (Corporación Latinobarómetro, 2024, p. 1).

Table 4.2 Sources of discontent, 2023 (in %)

Countries	*Dissatisfaction with democracy*[a]	*Oligarchic government*[b]	*Distrust in the police*[c]
Argentina	60.5	84.3	61.5
Bolivia	75.1	70.6	80.0
Brazil	65.5	54.2	50.9
Chile	69.8	83.7	40.1
Colombia	79.8	77.0	55.8
Ecuador	87.0	85.3	72.7
Mexico	60.7	58.8	68.7
Paraguay	79.2	89.7	68.7
Peru	90.8	90.3	67.6
Uruguay	38.6	61.6	36.4
Venezuela	83.6	77.7	78.0
LAT-11	71.9	75.7	71.9

Source: Latinobarómetro Online Analysis

[a]Proportion of people "not very" or "not at all" satisfied with democracy

[b]Share of people who believed they are ruled by a few powerful groups which act in their own interest

[c]Share of people with "little" or "no trust" in the police

Even though rulers engage in abuses of power (corruption and/or excessive repression) and political parties and leaders develop opportunistic behaviors, democracy tends to persist in a low-level equilibrium in semi-patrimonial states. Elites obtain relatively strong security, with a combination of repressive structures of the past and frozen regressive tax deals (UNDP, 2021), while masses channel their demands through new forms of political participation, and, above all, through periodic protests when co-optation of poor constituencies ceases to work (López, 2018). In these low-intensity and unequal democracies, the civil service (bureaucracy, security forces, and judiciary and electoral authorities) tends to lend itself to political abuses. The influence of collusive practices on elections (including the buying of votes; see Justesen & Manzetti, 2023) is so widespread that only in two countries (Uruguay and Chile) do those who believe that elections are fair (75 percent and 72 percent, respectively) exceed the regional average of those who believe elections are fraudulent (62 percent) (Corporación Latinobarómetro, 2024, p. 77).

The state must be framed in the context of the lively debate about the developmental state. We must look at the inability to build developmental compacts around the developmental state as an endogenous institution, to understand the failure of the Latin American countries to reduce the gap with developed countries (Bizberg, 2021; Domínguez, 2023a). If the developmental state is considered a "hard state" (Wade, 2019, p. 490), I propose to measure the specificity of the Latin American state against that benchmark because its main characteristic is "weakness" (Faletto, 1989, p. 71). This attribute also connects with Gunnar Myrdal's institutional concept of the "soft state" prevalent in underdeveloped regions of the world (Myrdal, 1973). If a hard developmental state combines exclusive political institutions with socio-economic institutions that are inclusive, a soft state combines inclusive political institutions with exclusive socio-economic institutions, as is the case with most states in Latin America and the Caribbean (LAC).

For Myrdal (1979), soft states are led by governments that do not have the willingness or ability to do what is necessary in the pursuit of development objectives because they can neither resist nor coerce powerful vested interests. Soft states are usually controlled by corrupt, rent-seeking elites who are uninterested in economic policies that might bring widespread gains in welfare, perpetuating a trap of corruption and inequality. Myrdal's conclusion is that the "upper class elite" only "relinquished its privileges and opened up its monopolies" by "pressure from below" (p. 39).

Actors and Constellations of Interests: Squaring the Circle

In a political economy analysis of the actors and constellations of interests, the critical question is how coalitions can be built that can overcome resistance to change. This entails taking into account institutional context, power relations, and different values, interests, and preferences among the actors involved. The second wave of progressive Latin American governments, which began with the election of Andrés Manuel López Obrador in Mexico in 2018, has a monumental task ahead. Due to the structural problems of how to manage power relations between the actors, two elements absent during the first wave are currently added: (1) the extreme political (ideological) and affective (emotional) polarization fueled by social media, biased toward the far right coordinated with the Musk-Trump disruptive machine (Nunes, 2024); and (2) the weakness of parliamentary majorities, except in the case of Claudia Sheinbaum in Mexico (Ellner, 2024; Kessler & Vonmaro, 2024; Sarsfield et al., 2024).

Following the strategic-relational approach of state theory, I conceive of the state as an arena of political contestation between elites and state agents who control the infrastructural power (law, coercion, money, administrative technique, and knowledge-power) and progressive coalitions that attain political power thanks to the support of social movements. In this section, I analyze the triangular game between state, capital (elites), and labor and social movements, which determines the orientation of the state and government policies.

Because of the prevalence of state weakness, the critical point in LAC is how to move from the soft state toward a strong, developmental-environmental state capable of meeting rising expectations (Bizgerg, 2021; Duit, 2023). The state remains the most powerful actor in driving structural change, and its power lies in forging new alliances with groups and actors for the creation and distribution of rents and productive assets, within a democratic context where governments must mobilize resources to meet multiple demands that have fragmented rent-seeking. This complexity of interests has diminished the coherence and autonomy that the state must maintain while considering a diverse array of groups.

In contrast, the more cohesive capital has increased its power relative to labor and to the state itself in peripheral countries (Naseemullah, 2023). In Latin American countries this situation is exacerbated by the high levels of market power of a small number of giant firms, primarily diversified business groups (with a high share of family-owned firms), transnational corporations, and state-owned enterprises in the oil and mining sectors. Through their powerful business associations and other umbrella organizations, the private national groups—while exerting strong influence over public procurement contracts—often exercise veto power over policies that impact their bottom line (taxation, competition, or environmental regulations), by exerting pressure directly on the branches of government (the presidency and executive, the Congress, or the judiciary) and indirectly on intermediary bodies (political parties), or through control over the ownership of media conglomerates (UNDP, 2021; Adelman & Pryluka, 2024). The strong financial and media concentration provides the material and ideological foundation for that task.[2]

The experience of the first Pink Tide and the second—which is still under way— allows us to draw some lessons from the conceptual framework of the recent literature on the state–social movements relationship in the context of the debates on extractivism: the creative tensions between social movements and progressive governments (Ellner, 2022), the transformative effects of environmental conflicts or conflict transformation (Rodríguez et al., 2019; Domínguez, 2021; Al-Suwaidan & Mazaheri, 2023), and the different modalities of extractive bargains (Bowles & Andrews, 2023). This conceptual framework incorporates the intersectional potentialities of the dependency research program (Antunes de Oliveira, 2021) that were already present in the original work of Cardoso (1977).

Social movements have offered critical support to progressive coalitions. This has occurred during elections (except for a reactionary fraction of the indigenous movement in Ecuador), and throughout the terms of progressive governments, as shown in the last elections and periods of government in Bolivia, Chile, Colombia, Brazil, Mexico, and Uruguay. Against the all-or-nothing stance of the leftist critics of progressive governments, there is room for negotiation to share the costs and benefits of the green transition through green extractivism (see Chap. 3). That involves facilitating the empowerment and institutionalization (not

[2] In 2019, the assets of the three largest banks as a percentage of total banking assets were 63.6 percent in Colombia, 56.6 in Brazil, 49.4 in Mexico, 42.6 in Chile, and 41.4 in Argentina; https://www.worldbank.org/en/publication/gfdr/data/financial-structure-database. In regard to the media groups concentration see Media Ownership Monitor, https://www.mom-gmr.org/

co-optation) of social movements, in order to attend to their demands (Ellner, 2022). Progressive governments generally have been more receptive to the demands of social movements and less repressive of protests than neoliberal governments. But they must also leverage their political capital (the support of the social movements that helped them win the elections) to incorporate social movements into the policymaking process.

For their part, activists in social movements must learn that governing without sufficient parliamentary majorities requires concessions and sometimes pragmatic approaches in the management of political timing to achieve transformative policy decisions with enough support. Nonetheless, the danger of engaging in corrupt practices to get sufficient parliamentary support or to neutralize the aggressive opposition from a more hostile segment of the elite is ever-present (Ellner, 2023, 2024; Adelman & Pryluka, 2024).

Through a systematic use of conferences, councils, and sectorial and national dialogues, progressive governments must seize the opportunity to transform seemingly non-negotiable demands over environmental conflicts into a structured, open, and durable dialogue. Such a dialogue between social movements and Pink Tide governments implies a developmental state with a broad-based embeddedness style, to promote IGD transition through specific reciprocal concessions from decision-making to delivery (Villegas & Peña, 2024).

In this context, the concept of "extractive bargains" proposed by Bowles and Andrews (2023) allows for addressing the conditions of possibility for this transition. Extractive bargains are the way in which states seek to persuade various stakeholders and build consensus among multiple stakeholders about the necessity of implementing resource extraction policies for the greater societal good. The concept suggests that resource extraction is not only contestable but negotiable, and that all actors have some power (even though that power is asymmetric). Lastly, extractive bargains allow for building a normative conclusion: the road to an environmental-developmental state involves moving from social redistribution bargains (using the rents of extraction for poverty reduction) to bargains by a progressive developmental state with a focus on inclusive green structural change (Al-Suwaidan & Mazaheri, 2023). While negotiations must also include the extractive elites, it does not guarantee full collaboration, as the Chilean case shows (see Box 4.1).

Box 4.1: The Chilean Elites in the Green and Inclusive Transition

Esteban Valenzuela, a member of the Green-Social Regionalist Federation and the current Minister of Agriculture in the Boric government, and José Miguel Ahumada, a professor at the Institute of International Studies at the University of Chile and former Undersecretary of International Economic Relations in the Ministry of Foreign Affairs during 2024, stress the importance of institutionalizing dialogue spaces in the relationship between the government and elites, including them alongside social movements.

While Valenzuela highlights progress in the aim of "involving the private sector in the transition" through various dialogue spaces addressing environmental issues via negotiation, compensation, and the objective of job-generating development (Biodiversity and Protected Areas Service, Strategic Basin Tables, Peace and Understanding Commission, Sustainability Council, Innovation Council), both interviewees point out that the elite has drawn a red line regarding the tax reform (which aimed to increase fiscal pressure by four percentage points of GDP), which remains vetoed, despite the government's attempt to link the reform to competitiveness.

Furthermore, it seems that within the elite, there is some diversity, with groups from the agrarian sector, particularly exporters of fruits, wine, and olive oil, being more sensitive to the transition due to environmental requirements stemming from the EU's green protectionism, as well as the associations of small and medium-sized enterprises that produce for the domestic and Latin American markets. Meanwhile, the financial-media elite and transnational capital from the mining sector continue to show limited openness. The exception in this regard is the company SQM, which, following the approval of the National Lithium Strategy, eventually accepted an alliance with the state-owned company CODELCO, which is now the owner of 51 percent of SQM's shares. As a result, convergence funds modeled on European style have been implemented to compensate regions affected by extraction. Additionally, the financial sector might be encouraged to collaborate in the transition through the creation of a new national development bank (Agency for Development Financing, AFIDE), transforming CORFO in an independent public–private financing agency that has the support of the Latin American Development Bank (CAF).[3]

The Political Economy Conditions of Possibility: Some Light at the End of the Tunnel

Based on these relationships between the state, elites, and popular movements, it is necessary to discuss some general factors that delineate the conditions of possibility for escaping the middle-income trap and achieving IGD transition. For that purpose, I establish two assumptions, and a multifactorial argument based on the literature on distributive preferences, ECLAC's reports, the academic outputs of the epistemic community associated with that institution, and public opinion polls. (1) There is political will in favor of this transition, as evidenced by the fact that four of the five largest economies in LAC (Mexico, Brazil, Colombia, and Chile) are on this path (along with Bolivia and Uruguay, these countries account for two-thirds of the regional population and 70 percent of GDP). (2) The demand for policies supporting an IGD agenda (as expressed electorally) is influenced by the self-interested motivations of different actors and interest coalitions. Below I discuss the factors that, a priori, suggest support for the transition, the potential conflicts between them, and the social and economic dynamics that work against this objective.

Appearances Can Deceive: Factors Favoring Transition

Considering the main actors' values, interests, and preferences, I examine four factors that could support the pursuit of IGD: social stratification, rising expectations, demographic structure, and concerns about interpersonal and intergenerational inequalities. The good news: favorable prospects exist in the countries of the region (a broad base of potential electoral support) for an inclusive and green structural change agenda. This is

[3] Based on author interviews online on October 29 and November 15, 2024.

implicitly posited by ECLAC (2022) and is reflected in comparative public opinion surveys (Ipsos et al., 2024a),[4] provided that macroeconomic instability, and other phenomena connected with poor governance such as crime and insecurity, bad public services, or corruption, which are highly sensitive issues for the middle class, do not escalate (Busso et al., 2023; ECLAC, 2024b; Adelman & Pryluka, 2024).

The prevalence of low- and lower middle-income strata could be a supporting factor for an IGD, in a social context of high dissatisfaction. The current distribution of income is seen as unequal, there is not enough opportunity for decent employment, and limited access to quality healthcare and education, and the justice system or physical infrastructures are perceived as evidence of dysfunctional public services. These sentiments should, in principle, mobilize a clear electoral majority, assuming a correspondence between the predominance of low- and lower middle-income strata and the position of the median voter on the left-of-center spectrum (Guizzo et al., 2023). This hypothetical correspondence would align with the vast majority of formal and informal workers, two of the three main actors in the distributive conflict characteristic of primary-export economies subject to balance of payments constraints (Porcile & Sánchez-Ancoechea, 2021; Baker & Dorr, 2022). In LAC, 80 percent of the population were in a condition of vulnerability (low- and lower middle-income strata) in 2008, 75.9 percent in 2019, and still 76.4 percent in 2022 (ECLAC, 2023a, p. 68).[5] Such a condition is consistent with the dissatisfaction generated by high inequality.

The second factor that theoretically supports the transition is the general desire for quality public services, equality, better jobs, and protection of the environment. When the willingness to demonstrate for important issues is measured on a scale from 1 (not at all willing) to 10 (entirely willing) we find an impressive percentage in the 6–10 range (Table 4.3). These data show the importance of progressive values, some of them held

[4]In 2024, those who believed the cost of damages due to environmental pollution are much higher than the costs of the investments needed for a green transition were 68 percent for the three largest Latin American countries compared to 60 percent of G20 average (Ipsos et al., 2024b, p. 78).

[5]This objective stratification diverges from self-perception (subjective social class), in which belonging to the lower middle and lower strata reached 47.6 percent in 2023 across the RR-LAC, with the highest percentages found in the three largest: Brazil (57.2), Mexico (56.7), and Argentina (56.1). Latinobarómetro Online Analysis.

Table 4.3 Willingness to mobilize for specific causes, 2020 (in %)[a]

Countries	*Improve health and education*	*Combat abuse and corruption*	*Advocate for a more equal society*	*Improve wages and working conditions*	*Fight climate change*
Argentina	66.7	66.0	60.4	58.3	38.0
Bolivia	75.9	74.6	72.1	58.5	53.1
Brazil	78.3	72.8	71.3	73.7	52.7
Chile	56.9	55.8	58.5	53.7	49.3
Colombia	76.9	75.1	73.6	65.5	55.4
Ecuador	69.2	64.9	69.9	55.8	42.6
Mexico	45.2	54.8	57.6	49.6	37.1
Paraguay	86.0	83.6	81.9	79.3	49.8
Peru	75.8	74.5	74.5	62.5	53.9
Uruguay	61.6	61.1	63.4	48.6	38.4
Venezuela	63.4	59.4	59.7	53.6	34.5
LAT-11	69.7	67.6	67.3	59.7	45.7

Source: Latinobarómetro Online Analysis

[a]Share of respondents within the 6–10 range on a scale from 1 (“not at all willing”) to 10 (“very willing”)

by the middle classes, a group that has continued to consolidate despite shifts in the political and economic landscape.[6] In the same vein, as long as the provision of decent public goods remains unresolved, frustrated expectations will continue to grow, as shown by Latinobarómetro data on poorly or scarcely guaranteed economic, social, and environmental rights.

Nonetheless, “dissatisfaction of the middle-strata” (ECLAC, 2022, p. 28) is rooted in subjective perceptions of crime that are always higher than real incidence (1.8 times more on average across the 11 countries, ranging between 1.3 in Mexico to 3 in Brazil), in a context where three out of four Latin Americans consider that protection against crime is poorly or scarcely guaranteed, as the most poorly guaranteed right, with no exceptions.[7] This issue could become a hindering factor in the transition insofar as it fosters the rise of strongmen (Adelman & Pryluka, 2024) associated with authoritarian solutions and denialist policies. In addition,

[6]The combined share of the upper middle-, intermediate middle-, and lower middle-income strata evolved as follows: 27.0 percent in 2002, 36.7 in 2008, 41.4 in 2019, and 41.8 in 2022 (ECLAC, 2023a, p. 68). In terms of self-identification (subjective social class), the middle-class group represented 39.4 percent in 2013 and 40.7 in 2023. Latinobarómetro Online Analysis.

[7]Latinobarómetro Online Analysis.

Table 4.4 Most important problems, 2023 (in %)

Countries	*Economic and financial issues*[a]	*Crime and public security*	*Unemployment and other job-related concerns*	*Political situation*	*Corruption*	*Income inequality, social injustice*[b]	*Environment degradation, climate change*
Argentina	**40.7**	18.1	3.9	6.8	5.8	4.9	0.0
Bolivia	7.6	0.5	**25.2**	3.3	3.3	8.8	0.9
Brazil	10.5	6.2	**13.6**	10.5	4.5	5.3	0.1
Chile	20.0	**30.9**	5.0	3.9	2.2	13.3	0.2
Colombia	**22.2**	11.3	8.5	12.2	17.7	5.5	0.1
Ecuador	5.6	**47.8**	15.6	7.9	9.0	1.9	0.3
Mexico	**26.3**	24.9	12.9	2.1	7.4	14.8	0.4
Paraguay	10.3	6.3	**19.4**	11.3	16.8	5.2	0.2
Peru	19.1	8.8	3.9	**26.1**	17.8	5.5	0.7
Uruguay	14.9	**22.3**	17.3	6.6	0.8	5.0	1.8
Venezuela	**50.8**	1.3	11.6	13.5	1.1	0.2	0.0
LAT-11	**20.7**	16.2	12.8	9.5	7.8	6.4	0.3

Source. Latinobarómetro Online Analysis

Boldface: Most poorly guaranteed right by country

[a]Includes inflation and its proxy "everything very expensive"

[b]Includes poverty

Table 4.5 Priority to fight against climate change, by age group, 2023 (in %)

Countries	*Intolerance to inequality*[a]			*Priority to fight against climate change*		
	15–25	*61 and over*	*Difference*	*15–25*	*61 and over*	*Difference*
Argentina	70.3	74.2	−3.9	63.5	47.6	15.9
Bolivia	39.7	41.4	−1.7	63.2	50.0	13.2
Brazil	55.5	48.2	7.3	65.6	51.8	13.8
Chile	87.9	84.3	3.6	55.8	68.7	−12.9
Colombia	56.0	39.1	16.9	73.0	68.1	4.9
Ecuador	48.6	44.1	4.5	67.2	45.8	21.4
Mexico	40.1	45.2	−5.1	55.5	54.1	1.4
Paraguay	54.4	56.3	−1.9	54.2	57.0	−2.8
Peru	52.5	39.8	12.7	65.1	52.6	12.5
Uruguay	32.1	31.5	0.6	77.5	72.3	5.2
Venezuela	35.3	37.4	−2.1	59.3	61.5	−2.2
LAT-11	51.3	50.5	0.8	63.1	58.5	4.6

Source: Latinobarómetro Online Analysis

[a] Respondents within the 1–4 range from the scale 1 ("completely unacceptable") to 10 ("completely acceptable")

crime and public insecurity were considered the second most important problem across our 11 countries (11 RR-LAC), behind the most sensitive issue (economic and financial issues, included inflation), although with some variations by countries (Table 4.4).

The third seemingly favorable factor is a demographic structure with still relatively young populations and a large potential demographic bonus (ECLAC, 2023b). In 2023, a positive response to the statement "one must give priority to fight against climate change without considering its negative impact in economic growth" was generally predominant in the 15–25 age group and higher than among those over 61 years (Table 4.5). That should facilitate, at least in theory, institutional changes necessary for social and technological innovations for an IGD transition. Intolerance of inequality (a dimension of inclusion) tends to be higher among young people compared to boomers (Table 4.5). Access to affordable public university education could be a key factor explaining the low percentages in the 15–24 group in Bolivia, Mexico, Uruguay, and Venezuela, with strong public universities, in contrast to those in Colombia, Peru, Ecuador, or Chile, where university systems are predominantly private.

Table 4.6 Concerns about interpersonal and intergenerational inequalities (in %)

Countries	*Years*	*Unfair income distribution*[a]	*Environmental protection over economic development*[b]
Argentina	2013/2011	68.3	79.8
	2023	90.6	**55.4**
Bolivia	2013/2011	56.7	75.8
	2023	67.1	**60.9**
Brazil	2013/2011	77.6	73.3
	2023	79.0	**57.7**
Chile	2013/2011	87.0	85.8
	2023	92.4	**63.9**
Colombia	2013/2011	83.0	84.4
	2023	**80.6**	**70.6**
Ecuador	2013/2011	36.5	72.3
	2023	78.2	**61.8**
México	2013/2011	75.9	80.7
	2023	**73.0**	**55.0**
Paraguay	2013/2011	87.8	84.4
	2023	**82.0**	**56.8**
Peru	2013/2011	73.6	79.3
	2023	84.7	**59.8**
Uruguay	2013/2011	60.2	73.3
	2023	68.6	**73.0**
Venezuela	2013/2011	54.0	68.5
	2023	83.5	**61.5**
LAT-11	2013/2011	69.5	77.9
	2023	80.0	**61.8**

Source: Latinobarómetro Online Analysis
[a]Share of people responding "very unfair" or "unfair"
[b]Share of people responding "priority should be given to environmental protection"

Similarly, with respect to climate change (the green dimension of transition), the demand for sustainable development is higher among younger populations (those who will face the worst consequences of global warming in 2050 if the necessary measures are not taken now) than among middle-aged and older adults.[8]

[8] In 2020, public belief in climate emergency was in the under 18 age group was 70 percent in Chile, 69 in Brazil, 66 percent in Ecuador, and 63 percent in Argentina. Meanwhile in the group of 60 and above it was 49 percent in Chile, 51 percent in Brazil, 45 percent in Ecuador, and 44 percent in Argentina (Flynn & Yamasumi, 2021, pp. 57–58).

The last and fourth factor is the strong concern about interpersonal and intergenerational inequalities. This would support a progressive consensus in favor of developmental environmentalism, although always subordinated to the goal of reducing inequality, with the sole exception of Uruguay, where the data suggest that environmental protection could take priority. In 2023, 80 percent of the population across RR-LAC considered income distribution to be unfair or very unfair, a concern that has increased almost universally since 2013, the year when the historical series on this topic hit its lowest point (Table 4.6). In 2024, those who think that the world needs to act immediately (next decade) and take major action to reduce carbon emissions made up, on average, 84 percent in Mexico, Brazil, and Argentina versus 71 percent in the G20 (Ipsos et al., 2024b, p. 80). In addition, although support for prioritizing environmental protection over economic development has declined since its peak in 2011, a higher share of the population in most countries still considered combating climate change more important than economic growth, even at the expense of it, in 2023 (Table 4.6).[9] The increase in concern about income inequality is particularly striking in Argentina, Ecuador, and Venezuela.

Nevertheless, these two issues related to inequalities are overshadowed by other key problems and remain far behind economic and financial issues, crime and public security, unemployment and other job-related concerns, the political situation, or corruption (Table 4.4).

These results have implications for the feasibility of an IGD transition. First and foremost, when people think of all the different problems together, inclusion and environment are generally at the bottom (see Table 4.4), and economic concerns and crime dominate. It underscores the importance of using policy measures that can generate win-win-win outcomes between the triple challenge of productivity-enhancing structural change, social inclusion, and sustainability (see Chap. 1). Second, the demand for inclusive development is significantly more urgent than the demand for green development (see Tables 4.5 and 4.6). Although they do not have to be competing demands as there are significant synergies between them (see Chap. 1), adjusting that difference in perceptions will be a major challenge for progressive governments.

[9] In 2024, individuals in favor of giving priority to health and well-being of people and nature rather than focusing solely on profit and increasing wealth made up, on average, 72 percent in Mexico, Brazil, and Argentina versus 68 percent in the G20 (Ipsos et al., 2024a, p. 54).

Win-Wins and Social Class Dilemmas

Against the backdrop of the pulse of Latin American public opinion, these governments will have to resolve the contradiction between the logic of capital accumulation for structural transformation and the logic of democratic legitimacy in a context where vertical inequalities (defined by class) and horizontal inequalities (defined by ethnic, racial, gender, residential environment, and migratory status lines) significantly shape the distribution of the costs and benefits of extractivism and environmental protection (Alcañiz & Gutiérrez, 2022; Villegas & Peña, 2024).

Regarding class dynamics, the demand for inclusive development does not depend solely on the level of inequality (based on the assumption that individuals with lower incomes are more supportive of redistribution compared to those with higher incomes), but also on other factors that may interfere with this preference, such as tax burden, efficiency of the public sector, or macroeconomic imbalances (particularly spiraling inflation). At the same time, manipulation of anti-corruption sentiment by elites—those who also manufacture consensus about the poor as lazy, ignorant, and easily manipulated to justify their opposition to social policies (López et al., 2022)—can be used to delegitimize redistributive policies and exploit the fear of the "lumpen middle class" of losing status to those at the bottom in highly volatile economic and political contexts (Domínguez, 2023b, p. 148; Assusa & Benza, 2024).[10]

This helps explain the preference of the middle classes for a "low-taxation, low-redistribution equilibrium" (Guizzo et al., 2023, p. 16) and its shift toward the private provision of education and health. Thus, in a large survey across Argentina, Brazil, Chile, Colombia, Mexico, and Peru, 77 percent of individuals support progressive taxation. However, among the middle class, only 60 percent believe that those earning three times the minimum wage should contribute a higher proportion than those earning the minimum wage. Similarly, the majority support for increasing corporate profit taxes (two-thirds) significantly decreases (to less than 30 percent), when asked about expanding the tax base of income taxes to finance social spending, health, and education. Finally, support for social programs decreases from 50 percent in favor of non-contributory pensions to 40

[10] Such is the case in Argentina, where 66 percent believe that beneficiaries of social programs are lazy (Busso et al., 2023).

percent in the case of conditional cash transfer programs (Busso et al., 2023; Assusa & Benza, 2024).[11]

One reason why the poor do not expropriate the rich using the voting power of the majorities and why redistribution does not increase as countries democratize (Guizzo et al., 2023) is the extent of informality, a reserve army that conservative sectors use to divide the progressive bloc diffusing meritocratic ideology of entrepreneurship that alters the results of the expected distribution (supposedly the greater support for progressive taxation and increased tax burden among lower-income groups). Among middle classes such ideology would express a preference for inequality that is explained by the risk of downward social mobility associated with job instability, the widespread nature of informal working conditions ("uberization"), and the perceived threat of social advancement by those receiving assistance deemed unjust due to being undeserved (Panigo et al., 2019; Nunes, 2024; Adelman and Priluka, 2024).

For their part, the informal workers are highly susceptible to neoliberal rhetoric, or neoliberalism from below, which conflates rights (those of public sector employees and formal workers) with privileges, while simultaneously normalizing the privileges of the elite as unquestionable rights (Nunes, 2024). Informal workers do not feel themselves as beneficiaries of redistributive policies; on the contrary, they consider intents to expand the fiscal base at their expense as a threat (Assusa & Benza, 2024). Similarly, such class dynamics would explain why among individuals in the bottom income decile, 44.8 percent are not in favor of increasing conditional cash transfer programs, and 55.7 are against expanding non-contributory pensions, even though they could be potential present or future beneficiaries (Busso et al., 2023). Hence the importance of ensuring that informal workers—the forgotten people in environmental mobilization studies—are properly included in the design and implementation of just transition policies (Pucheta et al., 2023).

The progressive bloc's internal divide between class and horizontal divisions complicates the agenda to end extractivism, further intensified by

[11] Argentina, the second country with the highest tax burden (32.2 percent in 2021) in Latin America and the economy that redistributes income more, shows the least support among the six analyzed countries for the progressivity of taxes and for any formula aimed at increasing revenue to finance social spending and public investment in education and healthcare. At the opposite extreme, Chile, with a lower tax burden (22.2 percent) and among the most wealth unequal in the region, exhibits the highest support for tax progressivity and for increasing taxes to finance social spending and public services.

the elites' cultural war. This elite uses as fuel the moral panic and status anxiety of those who resent the symbolic or material achievements of certain minority groups and the poor, and those who are distressed by the decline in their standard of living and the prospect of no longer enjoying the rights they once had (Nunes, 2024; Goldstein, 2024). With the rejection of all distributive policies, especially those in favor of recognition of women's rights, indigenous movements, or Afro-descendants, cultural wars serve to defend traditional social hierarchies expanding the popular base of the far-right toward informal sector workers—through the meritocratic ideology of entrepreneurship, which obscures the inequality of opportunities that benefits the elites (Nunes, 2024).

Final Remarks

The previous discussion shows that, despite the social contradictions generated by increasing vulnerability and a large informal economy, there are elements to articulate a coalition of the willing in favor of an IGD transformation, which leverages synergies between productivity-enhancing structural change, social inclusion, and energy transition. Certainly, the conditions of possibility are not the same in all countries in terms of state capacities, social capital, levels of inequality and informality, and pragmatic leadership. If state capacities are intersected with unmet social demands, there are some clear candidates to lead the transition, such as Uruguay and Chile, while others, such as Venezuela, Bolivia, Ecuador, or Paraguay, appear to be more problematic candidates, with Brazil, Colombia, or Mexico remaining in between.

But to avoid falling behind, it is essential that all countries enhance and green the state. Latin American governments cannot remain detached from the movement to rebuild state capacities necessary to guide businesses toward resilient value chains and the green transition: a movement that has begun in the West to counter competition from China's environmental-developmental state (see Chap. 2). The key is to realign state–business relations, and, once again, strengthen the state's capacities for effective planning to reorient the goals of development with "a political action supported by the mobilization of heterogeneous masses and capable of being directed toward long-term objectives," to put it in the words of the Brazilian father of the dependency research program, Celso Furtado (1966, p. 390). Progressive governments, with the support of new developmental-environmental coalitions, and without leaving informal urban and rural workers behind, need to advance a new generation of green industrial policies by seizing the opportunity presented by the geopolitical crisis (the new great power competition) and a coordinated response to the climate crisis.

References

Adelman, J., & Pryluka, P. (2024). América Latina: la siguiente transición. *New Left Review, 149*, 151–178.

Albertone, B. (2025). Lost principles of a "sustainable developmentalism". *Review of International Political Economy, 32*(3), 766–789, https://doi.org/10.1080/09692290.2024.2447735

Alcañiz, I., & Gutiérrez, R. A. (2022). *The distributive politics of environmental protection in Latin America and the Caribbean*. Cambridge University Press. https://doi.org/10.1080/09692290.2024.2447735

Allan, B. B. (2024). Industrial policy and the green state: Forging a world after growth. *Review of International Studies*. https://doi.org/10.1017/S0260210524000421

Al-Suwaidan, M., & Mazaheri, N. (2023). Chapter 30: Natural resources and the politics of distribution. In J. Sowers, S. D. Vandeveer, & E. Weinthal (Eds.), *The Oxford handbook of comparative environmental politics*. Oxford University Press.

Antunes de Oliveira, F. (2021). Chapter 5: Who are the super-exploited? Gender, race, and the intersectional potentialities of dependency theory. In A. Madariaga & S. Palestini (Eds.), *Dependent capitalisms in contemporary Latin America and Europe*. Palgrave Macmillan. https://doi.org/10.1007/978-3-030-71315-7_5

Antunes de Oliveira, F. (2022). Bourgeois dependency theory and the forgotten roots of neodevelopmentalism. *Latin American Perspectives, 49*(1), 33–56. https://doi.org/10.1177/0094582X21103734

Assusa, G., & Benza, G. (2024). Preferencias impositivas y desigualdad social. Actitudes hacia los impuestos progresivos en Argentina y América Latina. In G. Assusa & G. Bezna (coords.) *América Latina Desigual. Preguntas, enfoques y tendencias recientes* (pp. 177–203). CLACSO.

Baker, A., & Dorr, D. (2022). Labor informality and the vote in Latin America: A meta-analysis. *Latin American Politics and Society, 64*(2), 21–44. https://doi.org/10.1017/lap.2022.4

Bernal-Meza, R. (2020). Conclusion: China and Latin America in the global political economy: The development of a new core-periphery axis. In R. Bernal-Meza & L. Xing (Eds.), *China-Latin America relations in the 21st century* (pp. 253–272). Springer. https://doi.org/10.1007/978-3-030-35614-9_10

Bizberg, I. (2021). Chapter 6: The political economy of the post commodity boom crises in Latin America. In A. Madariaga & S. Palestini (Eds.), *Dependent capitalisms in contemporary Latin America and Europe*. https://doi.org/10.1007/978-3-030-71315-7_6

Bowles, P., & Andrews, N. (2023). Extractive bargains natural resources and the state-society nexus extractive bargains: On world, many bargains. In P. Bowles & N. Andrews (Eds.), *Natural resources and the state-society Nexus* (pp. 3–30). Palgrave Macmillan. https://doi.org/10.1007/978-3-031-32172-6_1

Bresser-Pereira, L. C. (2017). The two forms of capitalism: developmentalism and economic liberalism. *Brazilian Journal of Political Economy, 37*(4), 680–703. https://doi.org/10.1590/0101-31572017v37n04a02

Bresser-Pereira, L. C. (2019). Models of the developmental state. *CEPAL Review, 128*, 35–47. https://www.cepal.org/en/publications/44978-models-developmental-state

Bull, B. (2022). *Un compromiso social para el Antropoceno? Reacciones de las élites al Acuerdo de Escazú y las posibilidades de un Estado verde transformador latino-americano*. Fundación Carolina/Oxfam Intermon Documento de Trabajo, 7.

Bull, B., & Aguilar-Støen, M. (2015). Chapter 12: Conclusion. With or against elites? How to move towards more sustainable environmental governance in Latin America. In B. Bull & M. Aguilar-Støen (Eds.), *Environmental Politics in Latin America. Elite dynamics, the left tide and sustainable development*. Routledge.

Bull, B., & Rosales, A. (2024). Elite dynamics and china's influence in Latin America. *Development and Change, 55*(6), 1206–1229. https://doi.org/10.1111/dech.12861

Busso, M. et al. (2023). *Preferences for redistribution in Latin America* (III working paper LACIR series, 120).

Cardoso, F. H. (1977). Towards another development. In M. Nerfin (Ed.), *Another development: Approaches and strategies* (pp. 21–39). Dag Hammarskjöld Foundation.

Cardoso, F. H. (1980). El desarrollo en el banquillo. *Comercio Exterior, 30*(8), 846–860.

Cardoso, F. H., & Faletto, E. (1978). *Dependencia y desarrollo en América Latina. Ensayo de interpretación sociológica*. Siglo XXI Editores.

Cardoso, F. H., & Faletto, E. (1979). *Dependency and development in Latin America*. University of California Press. (Expanded and amended version of Spanish edition of 1971).

Chiasson-LeBel, T., & Larrabure, M. (2019). Latin America's changing balance of class forces: An introduction. *European Review of Latin American and Caribbean Studies, 108*, 87–107. https://doi.org/10.32992/erlacs.10564

Christel, L. G., & Gutiérrez, R. A. (2023). Chapter 26: Environmental mobilization in Latin America. Beyond the lenses of social movements. In F. M. Rossi

(Ed.), *The Oxford handbook of Latin American social movements.* Oxford University Press.

Clark, P., & Rosales, A. (2023). Broadened embedded autonomy and Latin America's Pink Tide: Towards the neodevelopmental state. *Globalizations, 20*(1), 20–37. https://doi.org/10.1080/14747731.2022.2032986

Corporación Latinobarómetro. (2024). *Informe 2024. La democracia resiliente.* https://www.latinobarometro.org/lat.jsp

Domínguez, R. (2021). Industrias extractivas y desarrollo sostenible en América Latina: ¿oxímoron o nuevo imaginario desarrollista? Autoctonía. *Revista De Ciencias Sociales E Historia, 5*(2), 405–437. https://doi.org/10.23854/autoc.v5i2.179

Domínguez, R. (2023a). Miradas estructurales sobre los extractivismos. In H.J. Burchardt, C. Gárgano & L. Christel (*comps.*), *¿De la sustentabilidad al desarrollo? Entre el extractivismo verde y la transformación socioambiental* (pp. 155–176). CLACSO.

Domínguez, R. (2023b). The political economy of the failure of progressive fiscal reforms in Latin America. In H. J. Buchardt & P. Fehling (Eds.), *Taxation and inequality in Latin America: New perspectives on political economy and tax regimes* (pp. 137–156). Routledge. https://doi.org/10.4324/9781003336686-9

Domínguez, R. (2024). Los dilemas del extractivismo para la transición al desarrollo. *Información Comercial Española. Revista de Economía, 934*, 119–135. https://doi.org/10.32796/ice.2024.934.7736

Doner, R. F., & Schneider, B. R. (2016). The middle-income trap. More politics than economics. *World Politics, 68*(4), 608–644. https://doi.org/10.1017/S0043887116000095

Duit, A. (2023). The environmental state. In H. Jörgens, C. Knill, & Y. Steinebach (Eds.), *Routledge handbook of environmental policy* (pp. 43–54). Routledge. https://doi.org/10.4324/9781003043843-5

ECLAC. (2022). *Towards transformation of the development model in Latin America and the Caribbean: Production, inclusion and sustainability.* Economic Commission for Latin America and the Caribbean.

ECLAC. (2023a). *Social Panorama of Latin America and the Caribbean. Labour inclusion as a key axis of inclusive social development.* Economic Commission for Latin America and the Caribbean.

ECLAC. (2023b). *Demographic Observatory, 2023. Population dynamics in Latin America and their effects on the labour force.* Economic Commission for Latin America and the Caribbean.

ECLAC. (2024a). *Natural resources outlook in Latin America and the Caribbean, 2023.* Economic Commission for Latin America and the Caribbean.

ECLAC. (2024b). In Economic Commission for Latin America and the Caribbean (Ed.), *Development traps in Latin America and the Caribbean: Vital transformations and how to manage them.*

Ellner, S. (2022). Introduction. Progressive governments and social movements in Latin America: An alternative line of thinking. In S. Ellner, R. Munck, & K. Sankey (Eds.), *Social movements and progressive governments. Creative tensions between resistance and convergence* (pp. 1–31). Rowman & Littlefield.

Ellner, S. (2023). Left government strategies toward business groups and the outcomes. The Mexican and Venezuelan cases. *Latin American Perspectives, 50*(2), 130–150. https://doi.org/10.1177/0094582X231153875

Ellner, S. (2024). Applying/misapplying gramsci's passive revolution to Latin America. *Monthly Review, 75*(5) https://monthlyreview.org/2024/10/01/applying-misapplying-gramscios-passive-revolution-to-latin-america/

Evans, P. B. (2010). Constructing the 21st century developmental state: potentials and pitfalls. In O. Edigheji (Ed.), *Constructing the 21st century developmental state in South Africa: potentials and challenges* (pp. 37–58). HSRC Press.

Evans, P. B., & Heller, P. (2015). Human development, state transformation, and the politics of the developmental state. In S. Leibfried et al. (Eds.), *The Oxford handbook of transformations of the state* (pp. 691–713). Oxford University Press.

Faletto, E. (1989). The specificity of the Latin American State. *CEPAL Review, 38*, 69–88.

Flynn, C., & Yamasumi, E. (2021). *Peoples climate's vote. Results.* UNDP & University of Oxford.

Fritz, B., de Paula, L. F., & Prates, D. M. (2022). Developmentalism at the periphery: Addressing global financial asymmetries. *Third World Quarterly, 43*(4), 721–741. https://doi.org/10.1080/01436597.2021.1989299

Furtado, C. (1966). Hacia una ideología del desarrollo. *El Trimestre Económico, 33*(131–3), 379–391. s

Goldstein, A. (2024). La internacional reaccionaria y su influjo sobre América Latina. *Ecuador Debate, 122*, 163–178. https://ri.conicet.gov.ar/handle/11336/244506

Guizzo, M., Scarstascini, C., & Tommasi, M. (2023). *The political economy of redistribution and (in) efficiency in Latin America and The Caribbean* (IDB working paper series, 0152).

Ipsos et al. (2024a). *Earth for all survey 2024. G20+ global report: Attitudes to political and economic transformation.* Ipsos, Earth4All and the Global Commons Alliance.

Ipsos et al. (2024b). *Global commons survey 2024. G20 + global report: Attitudes to planetary stewardship and segmentation.* Ipsos, Earth4All and the Global Commons Alliance.

Justesen, M. K., & Manzetti. (2023). Poverty, partisanship, and vote buying in Latin America. *Latin American Politics and Society, 65*(3), 1–19. https://doi.org/10.1017/lap.2022.66

Kastelli, I., Mamica, L., & Lee, K. (2023). New perspectives and issues in industrial policy for sustainable development: From developmental and entrepreneurial to environmental state. *Review of Evolutionary Political Economy, 4*(1), 1–25. https://doi.org/10.1007/s43253-023-00100-2

Kessler, G., & Vonmaro, G. (2024). ¿Cómo se organiza el descontento en América Latina? Polarización, malestar y liderazgos divisivos. *Nueva Sociedad, 310*, 91–105.https://nuso.org/articulo/310-como-se-organiza-el-descontento-en-america-latina/

Larsen, M. (2024). How to integrate the Global South into the "green state" concept. *Third World Quarterly, 45*(11), 1777–1792. https://doi.org/10.1080/01436597.2024.2366398

López, M. (2018). States, elites, and inequality in Latin America. *Sociology Compass, 12*(8) e12598, 1–14. https://doi.org/10.1111/soc4.12598

López, M. (2020). State segmentation and democratic survival in Latin America. *American Behavioral Scientist, 64*(9), 1242–1270. https://doi.org/10.1177/0002764220941244

Munck, R. (2022). Conclusion. The state, social movements, and political strategy in Latin America. In S. Ellner, R. Munck, & K. Sankey (Eds.), *Social movements and progressive governments. Creative tensions between resistance and convergence* (pp. 283–298). Rowman & Littlefield.

Munck, G. L. (2024). The state as a determinant of democracy: Durable poor-quality democracies in contemporary Latin America. *Democratization, 31*(2), 341–365. https://doi.org/10.1080/13510347.2023.2267992

Myrdal, G. (1973). *Against the stream. Critical essays on economics.* Palgrave Macmillan.

Myrdal, G. (1979). Underdevelopment and the evolutionary imperative. *Third World Quarterly, 1*(2), 24–42.

Naseemullah, A. (2022). Dependent development in the twenty first century. *Third World Quarterly, 43*(9), 2225–2243. https://doi.org/10.1080/01436597.2022.2089104

Naseemullah, A. (2023). The political economy of national development: A research agenda after neoliberal reform? *World Development, 168*, 106269, 1–15. https://doi.org/10.1016/j.worlddev.2023.106269.0305-750

Nunes, R. (2024). *Bolsonarismo y extrema derecha global. Una gramática de la desintegración.* Tinta Limón.

Oreiro, J. L. (2024). *Class coalition and political economy of new developmentalism: An essay in honour of Bresser-Pereira* (Working paper post-Keynesian economics society, 2411).

Panigo, D., Castillo, K., & Monzón, N. (2019). La preferencia por la desigualdad y el ascenso de los gobiernos de derecha en América Latina: una aproximación econométrica a la hipótesis de Dubet. *Cuadernos de Economia, 10*, 71–98. https://www.redalyc.org/journal/5123/512359395007/html/

Paus, E. (2020). Innovation strategies matter: Latin America's middle-income trap meets China and globalisation. *Journal of Development Studies, 56*(4), 657–679. https://doi.org/10.1080/00220388.2019.1595600

Porcile, G., & Sánchez-Ancoechea, D. (2021). Institutional change and political conflict in a structuralist model. *Cambridge Journal of Economics, 45*(6), 1269–1296. https://doi.org/10.1093/cje/beab028

Pucheta, M. et al. (2023). *Just transition in the Global South.* Perspectives from Latin America. *EUTI Policy Brief*, 2022.07.

Rodríguez, I. et al. (2019): Conflictividad socioambiental en América Latina. Aportes de la transformación de conflictos socioambientales a la transformación ecológica. *Cuadernos de la Transformación (FES)*, 3.

Rossi, F. M. (2023). Chapter 1: Multiple paradigms for understanding a mobilized region. In F. M. Rossi (Ed.), *The Oxford handbook of Latin American social movements.* Oxford University Press.

Rubio, B. (2023). Transición hegemónica y progresismo: ¿es posible lograr cambios estructurales? *El Trimestre Económico, 90*(4–360), 929–960. https://doi.org/10.20430/ete.v15i60.1875

Sarsfield, R., Moncagatta, P., & Roberts, K. M. (2024). Introduction: The new polarization in Latin America. *Latin American Politics and Society, 66*(2), 1–23. https://doi.org/10.1017/lap.2024.15

Thurbon, E., et al. (2023). *Developmental environmentalism. State ambition and creative destruction in East Asia's green energy transition.* Oxford University Press.

UNDP. (2021). Regional human development report 2021. In *Trapped: High inequality and low growth in Latin America and the Caribbean.* United Nations Development Programme.

Veltmeyer, H. (2023). From extractivism to sustainability: Scenarios and lessons from Latin America. In P. Bowles & N. Andrews (Eds.), *Natural resources and the state-society nexus* (pp. 31–50). Palgrave Macmillan. https://doi.org/1007/978-3-031-32172-6_2

Villegas, B., & Peña, A. M. (2024). Development, democracy, and dependence in the Southern Cone: Political coalitions, stabilizing mechanisms, and their hazards. *Review of International Political Economy.* https://doi.org/10.1080/09692290.2024.2380869

Wade, R. H. (2019). East Asia. In D. Nayyar (Ed.), *Asian transformations. An inquiry into the development of nations* (pp. 477–503). Oxford University Press.

Wainer, A. (2023). ¿Un Puente al desarrollo? Cambios en el comercio de América Latina con Estados Unidos y China. *Problemas Del Desarrollo, Revista Latinoamericana De Economia, 54*(213), 3–30. https://doi.org/10.22201/iiec.20078951e.2023.213.69938

Whitaker, D. H., et al. (2020). *Compressed development. Time and timing in economic and social development.* Oxford University Press.

CHAPTER 5

Navigating the Turbulent Waters of Strategic Competition to Implement an Inclusive Green Agenda

Rafael Domínguez

Abstract The chapter examines the external factors influencing an inclusive green transition, highlighting the volatile geopolitical and geo-economic context that has worsened during Donald Trump's second presidency. The analysis connects structural dependency theory with world-systems analysis to explain Latin America's weaker international power. Despite this, it is argued that national governments retain agency to pursue dependent development, using the geopolitical landscape as an opportunity for inclusive green development (IGD). For that purpose, the concept of 'development by invitation' is explored in the context of partnerships with the US, the EU, and China. The geopolitical dynamics of energy transition and the fragmentation of the global economy into regional blocs are presented as pressures on governmental agency. The chapter concludes by proposing that progressive governments in Latin America can navigate these challenges through active non-alignment, leveraging agreements with major powers to drive the IGD transition in the face of global strategic competition.

E. Paus, R. Domínguez, *Toward Inclusive Development in Latin America*, Palgrave Studies in Latin American Heterodox Economics, https://doi.org/10.1007/978-3-032-08588-7_5

Keywords Regional cooperation • Development by invitation • Imperialism by invitation • Partnerships • Green protectionism • Middle power • Active non-alignment

> *... the orientations defended by Beijing in favor of multilateralism, peace, non-intervention, development cooperation, and the fight against climate change align with key principles of Latin American and Caribbean foreign policies.*
> —*Carlos A. Romero et al. (2025)*

In this chapter, I explore the external constraints and opportunities for achieving an inclusive green development (IGD) transition, which stem from a highly volatile geopolitical and geo-economic context that has become dramatically more unpredictable with Donald Trump's presidency. I connect the centrality of the external factors of the structuralist dependency (see Chap. 3) with the empirics of world-systems analysis to understand LAC countries' weaker international power status. However, this conditioning situation and subordinate relationship does not negate the agency of national governments to pursue a strategy of dependent development. On the contrary, it offers a window of opportunity to achieve IGD.

To examine the conditions that make for such a possibility, I begin the discussion with the concept of 'development by invitation,' which is now relevant in light of the proliferation of partnerships sought by the US, the EU, and China. I then review the geopolitics of the energy transition and the geo-economics of fragmentation into regional blocs within the global economy as constraints or pressures on a government's agency. Finally, I analyze the conditions of possibility for progressive governments to drive the transition through agreements with the US, the EU, and China by developing an active and coordinated non-alignment strategy to navigate the turbulent waters of strategic competition between great powers.

The main message of the chapter is clear. Despite the geopolitical turmoil caused by US–China rivalry, as well as the new divide between the US and the EU under the Trump turmoil, the energy transition continues to present a window of opportunity that LAC countries must seize through an active non-alignment foreign policy, in a delicate balance to avoid being squeezed between Trump's tariffs and threats on one side and competitive pressure of Chinese manufactures on the other.

Development by Invitation: Who Invites Whom

The concept of "development by invitation" (Wallerstein, 1974, p. 14) refers to a model where developing countries rely on core countries to drive their process of structural transformation. In the context of an IGD transition, development by invitation presents both opportunities and challenges for Latin American countries. On the one hand, it facilitates access to financing and clean technologies, enabling the transition to sustainable models. On the other hand, there is a risk that decisions regarding development priorities may not fully align with local needs but rather reflect the interests of those providing investment.

The concept of development by invitation allows for revisiting the strategy of dependent development within the new geopolitical and geo-economic context of energy transition to formulate three key inquiries: Will some Latin American countries be able to join the chosen few leveraging mineral partnerships and other international cooperation agreements with OECD core countries? How many guests could be included? Will China have the right to extend invitations during Trump's imperial presidency?

Wallerstein's development by invitation, as hybridization of the dependent development branch of dependency research program (Vernengo, 2006), recognizes the possibility of dependent development through government agency. It also offers a progressive framework for those seeking to evade "imperialism by invitation" (Panitch & Gindin, 2012, p. 90),[1] or they will have to protect themselves from the old-style imperialism without invitation, as the Trump Administration threatens Mexico and Panama. The hypothesis of development by invitation changed the focus of Arthur W. Lewis' industrialization by invitation model in which underdeveloped countries are "inviting manufacturers who are already well established in foreign markets" to initiate an industrialization process (Lewis, 1950,

[1] This term describes the adherence of neoliberal collaborator governments to institutions of informal American empire, such as international arbitration tribunals via bilateral investment treaties (Panitch & Gindin, 2012). Other recent manifestations of imperialism by invitation can be observed in the anti-nonmarket economy clause to exclude China, the return to the financial disciplines of the IMF, and the proposal to reinstall a US military base or to request admission to NATO (Barkin & Santarcángelo, 2024).

p. 38).[2] For Wallerstein (1974) the core countries are the ones that invite certain semi-peripheral countries. In any case, the late Lewis and Wallerstein shared the structuralist-dependency approach: within a core-periphery framework of international economic relations, dependent development may be possible.

Wallerstein's thesis refines the core-periphery model, which he related to the discussion of dependent development by Cardoso and Faletto through the concept of semi-periphery: semi-peripheral states function geopolitically as a sort of middle class of countries, stabilizing the world system. In their struggle to join the core through structural change and export diversification, semi-peripheral states have three strategies to achieve development in the "the new multipolar world of the 1970's" (Wallerstein, 1974, p. 21): "...the strategy of seizing the chance, the strategy of promotion by invitation, and the strategy of self-reliance" that Wallerstein considered a "left-wing myth" (Wallerstein, 1974, pp. 8–9, 25).

The strategy of seizing the chance involves aggressive state action to transform the structure of comparative advantages, starting from an already modest industrial base, which could be expanded when international circumstances (contraction of the center) are favorable. The second strategy, "semi-peripheral development by invitation" (Wallerstein, 1974, p. 14), is based on economic and political collaboration with external capitalists (as in the Brazilian miracle), coinciding with expansive junctures in the center. However, once under way, the change in cycle can lead to a center bargaining harder with semi-peripheral clients.

Based on Wallerstein's concept of development by invitation, other authors explored the dependent development of the semi-periphery, following the assumption that Wallerstein adopted from Cardoso (1972): dependent development could not be generalized to all peripheral countries. This was the case of Brazil, Mexico, and Argentina as opposed to Japan, Taiwan, and South Korea, the main beneficiaries of the geopolitics of the Cold War (Scheneider, 1999). The big LAC countries were not invited due to geographical reasons and the burden of history (the legacy of the Monroe Doctrine) being subjected, contrary to South Korea, to the

[2] Lewis acknowledged later the limitations of his strategy: the "periphery" response to the stimulus of the "core" did not automatically guarantee development, because the core–periphery relations were not only technological or economic but also political, as they hinged on the specific relationships between different metropolises and their colonial empires (Lewis, 1978).

induced debt crisis and the subsequent neoliberal deindustrializing discipline of the Washington Consensus (Pérez Caldentey & Vernengo, 2021).

Later, the idea of development by invitation included new cases (Germany at the beginning of the Cold War and China in its final phase; see Olivera, 2019). But the three LAC economies of Cardoso's dependent development did not benefit from geopolitics.

From the Latin American perspective other voices have advocated for industrialization by invitation more recently, although in the Lewis style. The concept of power-shoring, as revisited by the Development Bank of Latin America and the Caribbean (the old Corporación Andina de Fomento, CAF), aligns with this approach in the context of opportunities arising from the energy transition. Power-shoring has two meanings: (1) a strategy of selecting geographical locations that offer ample availability of clean and sustainable energy sources (and critical minerals) to produce and avoid trade barriers associated with a significant carbon footprint; and (2) a business strategy for productive relocation based on the growing awareness and demand for renewable and sustainable energy sources, as well as the search for cost-effective and environmentally friendly ways to produce and consume energy. Nevertheless, FDI power-shoring requires a favorable institutional environment (CAF, 2024).

How does this kind of power-shoring and development by invitation strategies fit into the classification of countries based on their ability to achieve an IGD transition? To answer this question, it is necessary to first analyze the new strategic competition among great powers which has triggered a Second Cold War, the geopolitics of energy transition to fight climate change, and the fragmentation into regional blocs of a world economy in a process of *slowbalization*.

Second Cold War and Geopolitization of International Economic Relations

Since 2017, when President Trump initiated the trade and technology war against China's new industrial policy *Made in China 2025* the world has been immersed in an emerging Second Cold War (Schindler et al., 2024). The clearest indicator of this conflict—understood as part of a longer historical pattern—is the surge of geopolitical thought, i.e., the influence of geographic factors on state political power in international relations. Following Russia's invasion of Ukraine in 2022, as a tipping point of the geopolitical turn, two rival blocs have been consolidated in the global economy. Marked by geopolitical shifts, the global ecological crisis due to climate change and the fourth industrial revolution with its energy transition backbone (Sachs, 2024) and the Second Cold War between the US and China will be the defining features of world politics in the coming decades. Compared to the First Cold War its distinctive economic features are interconnectivity and interdependence in the interrelated networks of infrastructure, digital connections, production, and finance (Schindler et al., 2024).

As a result of the historical process of uneven development between center and periphery, the division of the world economy and politics in a two-bloc hierarchy pits the Political/Global West (now internally fractured due to the division between the US and Europe) against the Political/Global East. The latter is formed by the alliance between China, a new core power and the senior partner, with Russia (the junior partner) and its own allies of the Eurasian Economic Union, backed by the Shanghai Cooperation Organization (SCO),[3] the BRICS Plus (Egypt, Ethiopia, Iran, the United Arab Emirates, and Indonesia), and BRICS partners.[4]

Like in the First Cold War, the two blocs are intensifying their competition for influence in the Global South. China belongs to this grouping in its capacity as a major developing (upper middle-income) country (Tran, 2024a), and, at the same time, presents a global economic and political powerhouse alternative to Western hegemony leading the Global South. Nevertheless, as a "hybrid superpower" (Zhao, 2024, p. 168), Beijing has the expectation to replace US hegemony with a new Chinese hegemony, a Western concept alien to China's millennia-old tradition in international relations. This stance is evidenced by China's commitment to "embedded globalization" (Vadell & Jabbour, 2024), through its three global initiatives (development, security, and civilization), unified under the slogan *the community with a shared future for humanity* rooted in the Five Principles of Pacific Coexistence of Bandung (Domínguez, 2023; Enfu & Xia, 2024). Under the umbrella of South-South cooperation, these three soft power initiatives complement the hard Belt and Road Initiative (BRI),

[3] Belarus, China, India, Iran, Kazakhstan, Kyrgyzstan, Pakistan, Russia, Tajikistan, and Uzbekistan.

[4] Algeria, Belarus, Bolivia, Cuba, Indonesia, Kazakhstan, Malaysia, Nigeria, Thailand, Turkey, Uganda, Uzbekistan, and Vietnam. In 2024, Venezuela failed in its bid to join this second tier after Brazil vetoed its admission in the XVI BRICS Summit of Kazan. In 2025, Indonesia become a full member of BRICS Plus.

which includes 155 countries, 23 of them from LAC. Among our 11 countries, eight signed BRI MOUs with China: Uruguay, Bolivia, Chile, Venezuela, and Ecuador in 2018; Peru in 2019; Argentina in 2022; and Colombia in 2025.[5] In this South-South cooperation framework, Chinese initiatives prioritize tangible benefits in terms of trade, development finance, and technology transfer, and they represent a pragmatic approach based on results. That stands in contrast to the Western emphasis on principles, values and ideology promoted by a Western minority (Zhou, 2024; Zhao, 2024; Ishmael, 2024); however, this is changing rapidly with the second Trump Administration.

A framework of cooperation is the basis for the latest proposal to create a Global South Green Development Plan by Yiping Huang, the academic heir of Justin Yifu Lin at Peking University, whose Global Infrastructure Initiative (formulated in 2009) was the precursor of the BRI. It aims to facilitate the energy transition in the Global South, leveraging China's technological and financial capabilities, while simultaneously stabilizing China's growth trajectory (Yiping, 2024). The assumption that this strategy would be shared with European countries and Bretton Woods institutions (IMF and World Bank) anticipates some of the international realignments yet to come.

Thus, like with the 1970s surge of the geopolitics of energy, the analysts' consensus is that the international system will become increasingly multi-centered and ideologically pluralistic in the coming years, despite the division into blocs (Sachs, 2024; Zhao, 2024; Zhou, 2024). US and key European countries, having lost their moral appeal due to their support of Israel's ethnic cleansing operations in Gaza, will no longer hold the monopoly on rule-setting norms (the 'rules-based order' driven by Washington), which states in the Global South perceive as a blatant practice of double standards. Meanwhile, countries in the Global South, for whom sanctions against Russia were a tipping point prompting an independent trajectory, will try to strengthen their agency by taking steps to play a more assertive role in shaping the global landscape and claiming their right to development (Tran, 2025). Some of these shared goals are the promotion of multilateral frameworks representative of today's

[5] https://greenfdc.org/countries-of-the-belt-and-road-initiative-bri/. In October 2024, Colombia announced its accession process to the BRI, alongside its membership as a partner of the New Development Bank, which is expected to take place in July 2025 during the BRICS Summit in Rio de Janeiro.

diffusion of power (BRICS Plus and BRICS partners); the defense of a world order grounded in international law and the United Nations Charter; and leveraging raw-material wealth (reserves of hydrocarbons and critical minerals) to foster value addition domestically through partnerships that enable an ascent up the supply chains.

Leaving aside the de-industrialization process of the periphery, the division into geopolitical-trading blocs of the world economy and politics has its material basis in the critical minerals required for the fourth industrial revolution, the clean technologies of the energy transition—like wind turbines, solar panels, EVs, and energy storage systems—and modern military technology (Vivoda, 2023; Hendrix, 2023; ECLAC, 2024b). These systems account for the lion's share (60 percent) of the demand for critical minerals; thus, automotive companies will take up the lead positions in global production networks (Bridge & Faigen, 2022). Although the energy transition reduces dependence on fossil fuels, the production, refining, and processing of transition metals are more geographically concentrated than those of oil and natural gas (Martins, 2024; Victor et al., 2024). For the Political West, China has near-monopoly status in the supply chains of critical minerals (60 percent of production and 85 percent of processing capacity) that can be weaponized amid growing international demand and extreme price volatility. Thus, a strategy of de-risking supply chains from China is necessary (Vivoda et al., 2024; Victor et al., 2024; Draghi, 2024).

The US sought to win over LAC countries by granting them entry into new partnerships, such as the Minerals Security Partnership (MSP), established in 2022. Considered the NATO for minerals and metals (Vivoda, 2023), MSP comprises 15 like-minded partners.[6] It was trying to win over several Latin American economies to build a supply chain, an alternative to dominance of China in the processing of transition minerals, and of Russia along other BRICS partners and South American countries extracting strategic materials (Vivoda et al., 2024). For this purpose, Mexico, Ecuador, Peru, and Argentina were invited to the MSP High Level Forum in July 2024.[7] In the same vein, the US approached the countries in the region through other overlapping initiatives, although there have been no

[6] Australia, Canada, Estonia, Finland, France, Germany, India, Italy, Japan, Norway, South Korea, Sweden, the UK, the US, and the EU.

[7] https://policy.trade.ec.europa.eu/news/eu-and-us-welcome-new-members-minerals-security-partnership-2024-09-27_en

results to date (e.g., the Americas Partnership for Economic Prosperity of 2023), and their continuity is in question with the second Trump Administration's preference for a bilateral transactions approach (Romero et al., 2025).

But the costs of eliminating dependence on China are unsustainable in the short term. Also strategies such as re-shoring, near-shoring, and friend-shoring constitute a long-term approach (de Graaf et al., 2024), Therefore, the geopolitical game in the era of energy transition of the "new international energy power structure" (Yang et al., 2023, p. 684) is expected to be more symmetrical at the top (between China and Russia, on one side, and the US and EU, on the other) and, at the same time, multi-centered because the US and EU will have conflicting interests, and both, along with China and Russia, will seek to court Global South countries for their own benefit in a world without clear hegemony. Indeed, in the new world energy order, the Global South is the primary reservoir of critical minerals. Extraction and processing of those raw materials pollutes air, water, and soil, underscoring the need for a just transition to prevent the reproduction of the unequal exchange model between those who control capital and technology and reap the benefits and those who possess natural resources and bear the social and environmental costs (Brown et al., 2024; Martins, 2024).

Geopolitics and Geo-Economics of Inclusive Green Transition Under Trump Disruption

The landscape of geopolitical uncertainties will impose limitations on the state's ability to drive the development strategies (neo-developmental or social-developmental) for an IGD transition. Therefore, progressive governments will need to manage the potential conflicts in their international relations. And they should seize the window of opportunity offered by the increase in demand of critical minerals and the new role of state (vertical) industrial policies in the global restructuring of the value chains for development and environmental upgrading.

Based on their abundant endowment of resources critical for the green transition, the Latin American countries must learn to navigate bilaterally and in a coordinated manner on the increasingly unstable and fluid geopolitical chessboard. There is room for seizing opportunities to manage regional relations with China, the US, and the EU. Such a strategy of active non-alignment entails two elements: first, leveraging the opportunity arising from the presence of multiple players in the region as a contested arena, and second, adopting a new foreign policy approach that positions LAC countries themselves as key actors, although some will be more important than others.

In the strategic competition among the great powers, LAC is more a passive stage than an actor, and with respect to some countries, a vast repository of natural resources. To determine whether the region can transition from being an object to a subject, it is necessary to analyze the main actors in the dispute over Latin America's natural resources: the Political West and China. For the first bloc, Trump's imperial presidency will deepen the differences between Washington, with its new aim for short-term decoupling, and Brussels-Tokyo-Seoul, which favor a medium-term de-risking strategy (Crabtree, 2024).

In the context of geopolitical and geo-economic divisions between the US and China, Latin American countries will need to balance their alliances and leverage strategic resources, while facing radical uncertainty about their economic and geopolitical future. Nevertheless, the geopolitical turmoil is not necessarily bad for the Global South. Contrary to the IMF doctrine of the negative effects of the fragmentation of the global economy, other analysts believe that the network character of the rivalry between the US and China and the lack of international orthodoxy may increase the space, the "international permissibility" that Brazilian dependency theorist Helio Jaguaribe (1979, p. 97) spoke of, to implement autonomous development policies through a new non-alignment strategy (Schindler et al., 2024; Adelman & Pryluka, 2024). But the Trump Administration changes everything, affecting directly and strongly Latin American countries.

In this geopolitical game, Brazil is a key player in LAC, sharing with China a soft balancing autonomous strategy, with a high diplomatic profile. That is demonstrated by Lula's peace initiative for Ukraine and his condemnation of Israel's genocide in Gaza, while continuing to remain outside of like-minded US partnerships and the FTA system,[8] the Chinese BRI, the veto of Venezuela's inclusion in the BRICS partners, and its assertion as a middle power, underscored by its role as host of the BRICS

[8] Like India, Brazil is not a member of the Convention on the Settlement of Investment Disputes between States and Nationals of Other States that created the International Centre for Settlement of Investment Disputes (ICSID) belonging to the World Bank.

Summit in July 2025 and the COP30 in November of the same year (Tran, 2025). Despite its goal of climate neutrality by 2050 in the 2022 NDC, the country seeks to become the fourth largest producer in the world exploiting the pre-salt unconventional recoverable resources (SEI et al., 2023). Concomitantly, following the Chinese path (finance the energy transition with resources from hydrocarbons extraction), Brazil has become the main destination for FDI to emerging markets (China excluded) in the sector of renewable energy in the period 2014–2023 ($27 billion out of a total of $115 billion), with 23 percent of all renewable energy generation in emerging markets (excluding China) in 2023 (BloombergNEF, 2024, pp. 50, 59).

Nearly all of our 11 countries can be considered swing states: they maintain a strategic approach, choosing their alignment with the US (the political and military hegemon in the Western Hemisphere) and China (the main trade and development financial partner in South America) on a case-by-case basis. The only exceptions are Venezuela and Bolivia, as they are members of the Bolivarian Alliance for the People of our America (ALBA by its acronym in Spanish). None of them supported diplomatic and economic sanctions against Russia, with some simultaneously participating in US partnerships regarding critical minerals and the energy transition.

The case of Mexico is special too. It has become an "economic connector" (in Bloomberg's wording), since the trade war between the US and China has increased exchanges with both partners. And it has benefited from the growth of US investment in near-shoring and Chinese investment to circumvent American tariffs. Although Trump will leverage increased tariffs and domestic content regulations, curb migration, and block Chinese investment, the Mexican role as the guardian of Southern border migration could enhance its position as an economic connector in the USMCA renegotiation set for 2026 (Adelman & Pryluka, 2024).

Leveraging critical minerals for development allows for anticipation that the energy transition may result in potential winners or losers (Overland et al., 2019). The vast proven reserves of national oil companies (Petrobras, PEMEX, PVDSA, Ecopetrol, YPF, Petroecuador, or YPFB), which contribute more than 80 percent of the region's oil production (ECLAC, 2024c), may block any interest in the transition to prevent the problem of stranded assets (Stanley, 2020; see also Chap. 2). This could mean that several economies in the region face challenges in advancing the energy transition due to the vast reservoirs (conventional and unconventional) of oil and gas (Venezuela, Argentina, or Brazil), or due to their status as net energy exporters (Bolivia, Colombia, and Venezuela) (CAF, 2024).

With its nostalgic MAGA dream and bizarre transactional bilateral bargaining approach, the second Trump's presidency adds even greater uncertainty and geopolitical volatility to the international landscape, where geopolitical rivalry, geo-economic fragmentation, and *slowbalization* through the securitization (resilience by near-shoring or friend-shoring, and, above all, on-shoring) of global value chains are interconnected (Tran, 2024a; Tran, 2025). Focusing primarily on domestic issues to preserve or re-establish US technological superiority, Trump's ambivalent isolationist ideology will help escalate tensions with Xi Jinping's China dream of national rejuvenation. As the Trump *rapprochement* with Russia will concentrate the US competition with China, this will translate into stronger pressure to dominate the Western Hemisphere.

In light of what occurred during his previous term, Trump's geopolitical strategy and economic program will likely translate for LAC into less aid for development and more of it tied, more trade tariffs and domestic content regulation, and more discursive bullying of oil-producing states and countries with significant reserves of critical minerals, in order to prevent any alignment with China. Trump has his own Monroe Doctrine. But this renewed interventionist policy—with maximum pressure on countries to pick sides in the great power competition—could have the counterproductive effect of leading the affected countries to strengthen their ties with China. Nevertheless, whether the countries of the region shift toward China if they feel excessive pressure from the US will depend on how close the trade and financial relationships are with each partner and on the ability to sustain economic growth in the face of Washington's sanctions or its *ersatz* in the form of rising tariffs.

International Political Economy Conditions of Possibility

US Imperialism by or Without Invitation

With the second Trump Administration the owner of the backyard has returned to stay. So, the ability of countries more dependent on the US to diversify their economic relations with other actors will be a critical factor in strengthening regional agency.

The renewed big stick policy of the US could unexpectedly condition the relationship with China, but also with the EU, as demonstrated by the swift conclusion of the Mercosur Association Agreement in 2024 and with Mexico in January 2025 (Tran, 2025). In a world order with no clear hegemony, LAC's courting by China and the EU could mean more room for maneuver for some countries of the region in terms of increasing voice and the possibility to negotiate assertively with the US, but also more uncertainty (Hirst et al., 2024), based on the degree of commercial dependency and foreign investment of the US, EU, and China (Table 5.1).

In the first Trump Administration and subsequent Biden Administration, the prevailing response toward LAC partners engaging with China—seen as a vital threat to the security of US regional hegemony—tended to be positive inducements in the form of more aid for non-revisionist democratic states (Zelikovich & Yamin, 2024).

Under the new Trump Administration, Washington will use bilateral agreements with LAC countries committed to the strategy of imperialism by invitation and other like-minded ones to continue with the decoupling from China (Tran, 2024b). That is the Claver-Carone plan branded

Table 5.1 Trade and foreign investment relations of the US, EU, and China with RR-LAC

Countries	*US as trade partner*[a]	*FDI US*[b]	*EU as trade partner*[a]	*FDI EU*[b]	*China as trade partner*[a]	*FDI China*[b]
Argentina	4&3	3	2&4	1	3&2	2
Bolivia	7&6	–	8&7	1	5&3	–
Brazil	3&2	3	2&3	2	1&1	1
Chile	1&2	4	4&4	3	2&1	1
Colombia	1&1	1	2&3	3	3&2	6
Ecuador	1&1	1	4&3	–	2&2	2
Mexico	1&1	1	3&3	3	4&2	2
Paraguay	5&3	2	4&5	3	-&2	–
Peru	1&2	n.d.	3&3	n.d.	1&2	n.d.
Uruguay	5&3	3	3&6	2	1&1	–
Venezuela	4&2	n.d.	3&5	n.d.	1&1	–

Source: Atlas of Economic Complexity, ECLAC (2024a, pp. 69–72) and Dussel Peters (2024, p. 8)

[a]Rank market in exports & imports in 2022

[b]Rank market in FDI in 2020–2023

provisionally as 'Making the Americas Grow Again.' The plan is rooted in the *America Crece* strategy of the first Trump presidency and in the bipartisan and bicameral bill presented in March 2024 to the Congress known as the *Americas Act* (Claver-Carone, 2024; Katz, 2024). This bill aims to establish regional trade, investment, and people-to-people partnerships of countries in the Western Hemisphere to stimulate growth and regional integration through private sector development by on-shoring and near-shoring from China.

The bill, currently in the Senate Finance Committee for review, focuses on promoting partnership agreements with countries like Uruguay and Costa Rica as well as others under the Americas Partnership for Economic Prosperity, while excluding members of the ALBA (Cuba, Nicaragua, Venezuela, Bolivia, and some Caribbean nations). The US offers preferential market access and a Re-shoring and Near-shoring Account with up to $70 billion in public loans and grants to attract Western industries from China. This initiative also includes financial support for innovation and job training. It aims to foster rapid industrialization in the Western Hemisphere and reduce China's influence through large-scale infrastructure investment. It establishes the Build Americas Unit within the US International Development Finance Corporation (DFC) to offer credit to high-income countries in the region (e.g., Chile and Uruguay). Additionally, it allows for renegotiation of duty rates under GATT 1994 to counter goods that harm US industry.

EU Promises of Development or Another Turn of the Protectionist Screw?

In the context of the US exit from the Paris Climate Agreement and the division between the US and EU, the EU could be an ally supporting the energy transition in LAC. Countries could conclude partnerships with Europe for soft balancing against the US taking advantage of the EU's own interests (Table 5.2). For example, in April 2024, the European Commission approved the Critical Raw Materials Act which includes a 2030 target that no more than 65 percent of the EU's annual consumption of each strategic raw material, at any relevant stage of processing, should originate from a single third country (Tröster et al., 2024).

The European Commission (2024) has renewed its political partnership with LAC with the argument of leading together a fair green and digital transition. A significant development in this regard is the

Table 5.2 The influence of the US and EU on RR-LAC

Countries	*APEP*	*US FTA*	*EU association agreement*	*Minerals security partnership*	*Critical raw materials club*
Argentina			Regional (Mercosur)[a]	Invited to the HLF	MoU on SPSMVC
Bolivia			Regional (Mercosur)[a]		ERM chapter
Brazil			Regional (Mercosur)[a]		ERM chapter
Chile	x	x	Bilateral	Invited to the HLF	MoU on SPSMVC and ERM chapter
Colombia	x	x	Regional (Andean Community)		
Ecuador	x		Regional (Andean Community)	Invited to the HLF	
Mexico	x	x	Bilateral	Invited to the HLF	ERM chapter
Paraguay			Regional (Mercosur)[a]		ERM chapter
Peru	x	x	Regional (Andean Community)	Invited to the HLF	
Uruguay	x		Regional (Mercosur)[a]		ERM chapter

Sources: US Department of State, https://www.state.gov/americas-partnership-for-economic-prosperity/; US Free Trade Agreement Partner Countries, https://www.trade.gov/us-free-trade-agreement-partner-countries; EU Trade Relations by country/region, https://policy.trade.ec.europa.eu/eu-trade-relationships-country-and-region_en; EU and US welcome new members to Minerals Security Partnership, https://policy.trade.ec.europa.eu/news/eu-and-us-welcome-new-members-minerals-security-partnership-2024-09-27_en; Raw materials diplomacy, https://single-market-economy.ec.europa.eu/sectors/raw- EU-Mercosur partnership agreement, https://policy.trade.ec.europa.eu/eu-trade-relationships-country-and-region/countries-and-regions/mercosur/eu-mercosur-agreement/factsheet-eu-mercosur-partnership-agreement_en

[a]Under ratification; APEP (Americas Partnership for Economic Prosperity); ERM (energy and raw materials); SPSMVC (Strategic Partnership on Sustainable Raw Materials Value Chain)

establishment of a Critical Raw Materials Club to strengthen sustainable supply chains and diversify sourcing, bringing consuming and resource-rich countries together to jointly address the shared challenges. Such a Club will be composed of buyers, with a centralized purchasing mechanism, and sellers that have a strategic partnership with the EU, in order to achieve "economic development in a sustainable manner and support value chain creation" (European Commission, 2024, p. 8). To this end, the EU proposed finalizing the modernization of agreements with Chile and Mexico, as well as concluding negotiations on the Association Agreement with Mercosur.

The main novelty is the Global Gateway, the EU's mini-BRI, designed to mobilize €300 billion between 2021 and 2027 for developing countries (€45 billion for LAC) (Tagliapietra, 2024), aimed at addressing infrastructure investment needs as an incentive for strategic partnerships (but the majority of the investments have been concentrated in Sub-Saharan Africa). Brought before the EU-CELAC Summit in June 2023, the EU-LAC Global Gateway Investment Agenda includes a list of more than 130 projects selected by the Inter-American Development Bank and the Development Bank of Latin America, with a fair green transition in the European way as one of the main pillars. The promises of investment in renewable energy projects (solar and wind farms, green hydrogen promotion, fostering electro-mobility, and public transport focus on trains, metro, and electric buses) and hard infrastructure (modernization of the electricity transmission networks) are backed by the development of the green bond market to mobilize private capital. But the promotion of the local value chains based on critical raw materials is only mentioned in a generic manner (European Commission, 2023).

To see whether the new developmental rhetoric in the Critical Raw Materials Act translates into concrete actions, we have to look at the negotiations of the energy and raw materials chapters of the association agreements with Mexico, Chile, and Mercosur, which are legally binding. So far, beyond the environmental developmentalist narrative —compliance with environmental, social, and governance (ESG) standards; contribution to local value addition; technology transfer to promote circularity; responsible recycling of critical raw materials in producing countries— the negotiations only reveal that the EU seeks "to ensure preferential treatment, market access and investment opportunities for its corporations in resource-rich countries" (Müller et al., 2024, p. 13). In this sense, the Critical Raw Materials Club is more a buyers' club to attenuate global prices ("fair prices" as Mario Draghi says) through market power in favor of EU countries and their guests (US, Canada, Japan, South Korea, or Australia) than a partnership with mineral-rich developing countries (Hendrik, 2023; Draghi, 2024). In the same vein, the green protectionism of the EU Carbon Border Adjustment Mechanism could be a new case of "kicking away the *green* ladder" (Lebdioui, 2024, p. 12).

Similarly, time will tell if the memoranda of understanding for the establishment of strategic partnerships signed with Argentina and Chile in 2023,[9] or the projects announced in Argentina, Chile, Brazil, Colombia, Mexico, or Uruguay under the Global Gateway, turn economic opportunities into mutually beneficial realities, but skepticism is almost inevitable. Unlike the patient public capital of China's BRI, these initiatives depend on the willingness and mobilization of private investment even using a very modest factor of leverage of 3.4 (Tagliapietra, 2024). In addition, a portion of the supposedly promised fresh funds corresponds to rebranded projects already in the funding phase (Lewkowicz, 2024; Müller et al., 2024).

The Regional Deployment of China's Financial and Diplomatic Artillery

China's role as a leader in developmental environmentalism is a critical factor for the IGD transition in LAC and the rest of the Global South. In fact, China's environmental diplomacy has fostered a rich institutional framework at the global level, to move from theory to practice. The BRI International Green Coalition (BRIGC), the Global Clean Energy Cooperation Partnership (GCECP), and the Initiative of International Cooperation on Resilient and Stable Industrial Supply Chains (ICRSISC Initiative) stand out (Zhu et al., 2024).

The BRIGC was announced during the Second Belt and Road Forum in 2019 for greening the BRI, which Beijing now presents as the largest international cooperation platform and a global public good promoting connectivity and enabling BRI countries to better integrate into global and regional supply chains (MEE, 2024). The BRIGC was established as a non-profit international organization backed by China's leadership in global renewable energy production and EVs (including electric buses), as well as its significant contribution to global climate finance: China doubling bilateral funds between 2013 and 2021 (MEE, 2024). Its mission is

[9] Both can be consulted at https://single-market-economy.ec.europa.eu/sectors/raw-materials/areas-specific-interest/raw-materials-diplomacy_en. Before the UE-CELAC Summit of Brussels 2023, the EU launched the EU–Latin America partnership on raw materials inviting Argentina, Brazil, Chile, Colombia, Mexico, Peru, and Uruguay, but after the Summit this initiative was put on hold: https://www.mineralplatform.eu/about/the-partnership

to enable countries participating in the BRI to realize green, low-carbon, and sustainable development through policy dialogue.[10]

The GCECP emerged from the Global Development Initiative launched in 2021, a complement to the BRI; it currently comprises an informal group of 82 eligible countries for the Global Development and South-South Cooperation Fund ($4 billon). The GCECP seeks to promote the integration of clean energy industry to ensure sustainable energy security, as stated in an official concept note of 2022.[11] The document encourages all countries (member states of ASEAN, the African Union, the Arab League, the SCO, and BRICS are mentioned specifically) and international organizations (IRENA is the key partner) to join with the promise to boost the economic returns along the whole value chain of energy.

Lastly, the ICRSISC Initiative was launched in 2022 by China, Chile, Cuba, Indonesia Pakistan, and Serbia, with the support of Argentina, in response to MSP. The following year, the China International Supply Chain Expo (CISCE) was organized under the China Council for International Trade together with other Chinese initiatives on supply chain cooperation in APEC, ASEAN Plus Three, the G20, and BRICS. China urged all parties to eliminate non-economic disruptions in trade relations. In the Second CISCE (2024), five international organizations participated (UNCTAD, UNIDO, WIPO, ITC, and International Chamber of Commerce) along with 600 companies and institutions from nearly 70 countries (over 40 BRI partner countries). The CISCE released a Beijing Initiative to promote cooperation in industrial and supply chains (Ren, 2024).

After a decade of political dialogue in China-CELAC, the region has deepened its commercial, financial, and political ties with Beijing (see Tables 5.1 and 5.3). That has prompted reactive responses from the US (mainly the US International Development Finance Corporation in 2019, the Partnership for Global Infrastructure and Investment in 2022, and the

[10] During the Third Belt and Road Forum in 2023, the BRIGC, along with 15 other Chinese and international partners, launched the Green Investment and Finance Partnership. This new institution is a green project service design platform aligned with ESG standards, where China's major mining companies have leveled up in recent years with their Western counterparts (Deberdt et al., 2024), and it functions as an investment and financing preparation mechanism aimed at promoting green demonstration projects in partners' BRI countries (MEE, 2024).

[11] https://www.mfa.gov.cn/eng/zy/jj/GDI_140002/wj/202209/P020220928609247051343.pdf

Table 5.3 The influence of China on RR-LAC

Countries	*Political dialogue status*	*FTA*	*BRI MoU*	*BRICS status*	*AIIB*	*NDB*
Argentina	CSP		x	Invited	Member	
Bolivia	SP		x	Partner	Prospective member	
Brazil	CWSF		Synergy	Founder	Member	Member
Chile	CSP	Upgraded	x		Member	
Colombia	SP		x			Under negotiation
Ecuador	CSP	x	x		Member	
Mexico	CSP					
Paraguay						
Peru	CSP	Upgraded	x		Member	
Uruguay	CSP		x		Member	Prospective member
Venezuela	All-weather SP		x		Prospective member	

Sources: Ministry of Foreign Affairs PRC; Ministry of Commerce PRC; Green Finance and Development Center, Countries of the Belt and Road Initiative (BRI); Norton (2024); AIIB membership, NDB membership

CSP Comprehensive Strategic Partnership, *SP* Strategic Partnership, *CWSF* Community with a shared future for a more just world and a more sustainable planet

Americas Partnership for Economic Prosperity in 2023) and the EU (the Global Gateway in 2021 and the reactivation, after six years of delay, of the EU-CELAC Summit in 2023).

The key distinction between China and the Western countries is that Beijing, since the first CELAC-China Summit in 2015, has allocated public funds to address the needs of both parties under the mutual benefit framework characteristic of South-South cooperation: $20 billion for financing infrastructure projects (the Special Loan Program for China-Latin America Infrastructure Project), $10 billion for development projects (China-Latin America Production Capacity Cooperation Investment Fund or CLAI fund), and $5 billion for specific initiatives in areas identified by China (China-LAC Cooperation Fund or CLAC fund). The sole condition was to maintain the China-CELAC Forum relationship. Notably, this approach did not exclude countries maintaining diplomatic relations with Taiwan (e.g., Paraguay), a dwindling group thanks to

China's yuan diplomacy. In recent years, there has been a significant shift away from development finance (which peaked in the period 2011–2014) toward outward foreign direct investment (OFDI) which reached $46 billion during the 2020–2023 period (Ray et al., 2024; Katz, 2024).

Guided by the principles of flexibility, voluntary participation, and special and differentiated treatment, four China-CELAC Forums were held in 2015, 2018 (when LAC was invited to the BRI, as its "natural extension"), 2021, and 2025 (Morales, 2024a; b). The last China-CELAC Joint Action Plan for Cooperation in a New Era (2022–2024) contained numerous references to cooperation on energy transition, critical minerals, and technologies for the fourth industrial revolution,[12] in parallel with the deployment of the Digital Silk Road, launched across the region in 2017 (Arsentyeva, 2024). The new China-CELAC Member States Joint Action Plan for Cooperation in Key Areas (2025–2027) delves into those areas, with an offer of $9.15 billion in supplementary funding through the Global Development Initiative (Morales, 2024b). Awaiting the publication of the third White Paper on Latin America (after those published in 2008 and 20,216), the possibility of industrialization and technological upgrading by integration in BRI and other partnerships with China remains open in theory (Fernández et al., 2023). The question is whether it will also be feasible in practice as the Bolivian case shows (see Chap. 2, and Johnson et al., 2024).

The recent diversification of Chinese OFDI in the region will also play an important role in the effort to add value and knowledge to LAC exports to China, as well as generating new production capacities and new intraregional production chains in some key sectors. These include non-extractive activities (EVs manufacturing in Brazil and Mexico, light rail projects in Mexico, Colombia, and Chile, first HVDC 1.350 km transmission line in Chile); natural resource processing projects (lithium cathode production in Chile and Argentina, solar photovoltaic-making factories in Chile, solar plants in Brazil, wind farms in Argentina, hydrogen projects in Brazil, Colombia, and Uruguay); telecommunications projects (Huawei smartphones manufacture in Brazil); and trade in services for building or operating public infrastructure projects.

[12] See chapters 5 ("Industry and Information Technology the Action Plan") and 7 ("Energy and Resources"); http://www.chinacelacforum.org/eng/zywj_3/202112/t20211209_10465116.htm

Based on Latin American's natural resources and leveraging China's comprehensive experience in industrial chain and extensive project implementation, Beijing advocates for development by invitation for the region (MEE, 2024). Latin American countries benefited from Chinese demand and the supply of cheap clean goods for the energy transition (wind and solar power equipment, EVs, and electric buses), OFDI, and development finance. But they will need export diversification, in a context where petroleum may gradually diminish, while copper and lithium are to increase steadily as China moves toward decarbonizing its energy mix. Instead of accepting its subordination to Chinese trade priorities, now should be the time for LAC to take advantage of the flexibility of Beijing agreements (Katz, 2024). Especially for those countries aspiring to upgrade their manufacturing sectors considering a potential surge in Chinese industrial exports to the region as a means of offsetting the reciprocal tariffs imposed by Trump (Tran, 2025).

Will There Be Space for Active Non-alignment? The Imperative of Regional Coordination

In the global debate about the Green New Deal, with the Global South demanding a Green New International Economic Order and the creation of a Global Green Technology Bank, regional coordination will be the only way to advance in a progressive global extractive bargain (Bowles & Andrews, 2024). The autonomy to carry out an active non-alignment policy (Fortín et al., 2020) will be much lower in those countries for which the US is simultaneously the main trading and FDI partner (Colombia, Ecuador, and the special position of Mexico) than in those which have diversified relations with China (Venezuela, Peru, Bolivia, and indirectly Paraguay) or with the EU, China, and Mercosur members (Argentina, Brazil, Uruguay, and Chile).

It will not be easy for the progressive governments of Latin America to carry out an active non-alignment foreign policy. It will require resolute progress in regional coordination. This time, LAC cannot afford to remain on the sidelines of the regionalization process led by the fragmentation of the global economy.[13] On this front, China, as a defender of Global South

[13] The Regional Comprehensive Economic Partnership (effective from 2021) led by China in the Asia-Pacific and the African Continental Free Trade Area brokered by the African Union (that entered into force in 2024) are at the forefront.

multilateralism with its adherence to the Investment Facilitation for Development Agreement of 2023 in the WTO, could be an ally. At the same time, China's manufacturing overcapacity could be a challenge for those countries aspiring to structural upgrading (Tran, 2025; see also Chap. 2).

The procrastination of regional integration could be reversed by taking advantage of the context of near-shoring and regionalization of supply chains as the EU aim to de-risk from China. Lebdioui (2024, p. 62) talks of "climate-resilience environmental regionalism," i.e., regional strategies for specific low-carbon industries to help align demand-side policies to create higher and more stable regional market demand, along with other supply-side policies (knowledge sharing, region-wide certification for low-carbon products, pooling limited R&D resources). Regarding the regional integration for a just transition, the current conversation is recovering some concepts. Variable geometry is the most cited to advance regional integration at different speeds. In addition, it is the core of active non-alignment, a strategy of equidistance between the two competing great powers which advocates for multilateralism, the creation of resilient value chains to face the IGD transition, and regional coordination in global economic governance (Rosales, 2023; Fortín et al., 2023). However, such a strategic agenda is challenging even in the case of coordination among progressive governments, due to countries' different development levels, priorities, degrees of embrace of a developmental state, and dependence on the US.

To avoid picking sides in the US-China rivalry, the interest of the region lies in the defense of multilateralism. If the EU-Mercosur agreement becomes effective, the region would have a network of trade agreements with disciplines relatively harmonized, since all the countries are members of the WTO Agreement on Trade Facilitation. Such a framework could be applied to the commercial relations among Latin American countries, opening opportunities for the formation of value chains and productive convergence (de la Mora, 2023; Rosales, 2023). But there are two major difficulties with this reasoning. First, the question of whether the EU-Mercosur agreement will indeed be ratified, given the opposition of some key European countries (France, Italy, and Poland). Second, given multinationals' domination in the extraction of critical minerals, their interest in advancing higher value added activities in LAC only works in special circumstances (big markets and greater capabilities in Mexico and

Brazil; see Chap. 2). Therefore, much stronger industrial policy incentives will be required than the timid ones implemented thus far.

In addition, the coordination of Argentina, Brazil, and Mexico in the G20 establishing a regional consultation mechanism with the countries in the region (or with CELAC) before each meeting (Rosales, 2023) is off the agenda as long as Milei, with his strategy of imperialism by invitation, remains president. More promising is that Brazil and Mexico, as key actors in Mercosur and the Pacific Alliance, may stimulate the convergence of initiatives between both organizations. For their part, Chile, Mexico, and Peru, as members of the Asia-Pacific Economic Cooperation, could lobby to allow for the participation of Mercosur countries in the main debates (Rosales, 2023).

In any case, the question is how to build a stronger institutional framework by enhancing what is already in place, rather than starting over with ambitious but fragile projects, as happened with the Union of South American Nations' relaunch operation which was quickly aborted after Javier Milei's victory at the end of 2023.[14] Discussions between Brazil and Argentina were reactivated in 2023 to promote the new regional architecture. However, the proposed framework (the creation of a unified common currency, a payment compensation system, a common reserve and economic stability fund, and a regional treasury based on the Bank of the South linked to the New Development Bank) failed to move from theory to practice (Oglietti et al., 2023) due to the Milei factor and later to the Venezuelan elections (Maduro's factor) in 2024. In a region with an annual deficit of investment in physical and digital infrastructures around \$2.2 trillion until 2030, and net international reserves around \$850 billion that central banks placed in highly liquid investments with very low or zero returns, the establishment of a financial regional architecture through the Bank of the South should be a top priority (Katz, 2024).

Failing that, regional coordination, in the meantime, should be intensified crossing the river by feeling the stones. Such a coordination includes the Regional Tax Cooperation Platform for LAC (PTLAC 2023),[15] the Regional Agreement on Access to Information, Public Participation and

[14] The same can be said of the grandiose objective of deep integration within the Pacific Alliance, which, after more than a decade, has failed to exceed 4 percent of intraregional trade among Mexico, Colombia, Peru, and Chile, and has not achieved any of the objectives of the free movement of capital, services, and people, or the building of value chains.

[15] https://www.cepal.org/es/ptlac and https://www.cepal.org/en/notes/regional-tax-cooperation-platform-latin-america-and-caribbean-ready

Justice in Environmental Matters in LAC (Escazú Agreement of 2018),[16] and Renewables in LAC (RELAC 2019).[17] Other areas of coordination have to be intensified to strengthen the integration process through the development of regional suppliers, such as talent development, networks of researchers in science and technology, and infrastructure.[18]

Finally, the formation of an OPEC-like Latin American cartel for battery minerals is not just to increase prices but also to use the cartel's market power as a wider industrial policy push to catalyze investment in downstream processing and refining capacity in order to move up the value chain and avoid being relegated to primary commodity exporters (Hendrix, 2023). The cartel would be formed by Bolivia, Chile, and Argentina, the countries which launched the initiative in a CELAC conference in Buenos Aires in 2022. Other countries with significant lithium reserves, Mexico and Peru, expressed interest in participation, and Brazil joined the talks in 2023 (Ling, 2024).

But these countries' commitment to resource nationalism clashes with the institutional differences among the partners, e.g., the governance of lithium (see Chap. 2). In addition, a lithium OPEC would not be feasible without the participation of Australia, which account for around 50 percent of global production (Milanez & Dorn, 2024; Rubiolo & Fiori, 2024). The possibility of Argentina declaring lithium a strategic resource—which could lead to nationalization and a likely suspension of all concessions nationwide—appears remote, as long as Milei remains in office.

[16] https://observatoriop10.cepal.org/en/treaty/regional-agreement-access-information-public-participation-and-justice-environmental-matters

[17] https://hubenergia.org/es/relac

[18] That is the case of the Pacific Alliance Scholarship Program (2013), a successful platform of student and academic mobility between the member countries, with almost 3000 scholarships between 2013 and 2024; the IDB Latin American and the Caribbean Research Network (1991), with more than 300 research institutes and 500 experts of the region on social and economic development; the Network of Macro Universities of Latin America and the Caribbean (2002), which currently groups the 37 major public universities in 20 countries (more than 3 million students, and almost 240 thousand faculty teachers), to work in academic networks of training and research; and the IDB research on mapping transport infrastructures and logistic for building regional value chains (Granada et al., 2022).

Final Remarks

The world energy transition provides a "once-in-a-generation opportunity" (Hendrix, 2023, p. 7) for LAC countries, especially those rich in critical minerals and sufficiently large in terms of GDP and market size like Mexico and Brazil, to build a strong foundation for the IGD that has eluded many of them. To seize that chance, cooperation, coordination, and regional integration are more urgent than ever to build a Latin American value chain and a market for renewable energy and electromobility, e.g., EVs for private use and electric buses for public transport in big cities. Only through this approach can regional industrial capacities for battery production and their inputs develop via collaboration with the automotive industry in countries with established factories (Argentina, Brazil, Colombia, and Mexico).

During the Biden Administration, the US was sending a message that just transitions are for developed countries, not for the people of the Global South. Now that Trump has once again withdrawn the US from the Paris Agreement, the EU green trade policy could incentivize the transition, but it also keeps Latin American countries at the bottom of the value chains. In contrast, China has the industrial capacities and the political will to avoid adopting protectionism in the name of green and low-carbon development, under Xi's mantra of "establishing the new before abolishing the old" (Xi, 2024). And, as a more friendly norm maker, Beijing is moving quickly to invite "fellow Global South nations" (Wang, 2024) to join the path of green modernization with Chinese characteristics. China's official stance on Latin America is that the region needs fairness, justice, and mutually beneficial cooperation, not power politics, hegemony, or bullying (LAC is not anyone's backyard). Assuming that the elites abandon the easy path of extractivism to move up the value chain, time will tell if Washington's return to the big stick policy and the competitive pressure of China's industrial overcapacity will allow them to fulfill the aspiration to IGD.

References

Adelman, J., & Pryluka, P. (2024). América Latina: la siguiente transición. *New Left Review, 149*, 151–178.

Arsentyeva, I. I. (2024). China's digital silk road: Challenges and opportunities for Latin America and the Caribbean. *Vestnik RUDN. International Relations, 24*(1), 51–64. https://doi.org/10.22363/2313-0660-2024-24-1-51-64

Barkin, D., & Santarcángelo, J. (2024). The IMF and class struggle in Latin America: Unvelining the role of IMF. *Monthly Review, 76*(1), 49–59. https://doi.org/10.14452/MR-076-01-2024-05_4

BloombergNEF (2024). *Climatoscope 2024. Emerging markets power Factbook.* BloombergNEF.

Bowles, P., & Andrews, N. (2024). Global extractive bargains for green new deals. In P. Bowles & N. Andrews (Eds.), *Natural resources and the state-society Nexus* (pp. 307–331). Palgrave Macmillan. https://doi.org/10.1007/978-3-031-32172-6_14

Bridge, G., & Faigen, E. (2022). Towards the lithium-ion battery production network: Thinking beyond mineral supply chains. *Energy Research & Social Science, 89*(102659), 1–19. https://doi.org/10.1016/j.erss.2022.102659

Brown, D., Zhou, R., & Sadam, M. (2024). Critical minerals and rare earth elements in planetary just transition: An interdisciplinary perspective. *The Extractive Industries and Society,* 19, 101510, 1–9. https://doi.org/10.1016/j.exis.2024.101510

CAF. (2024). *Renewed energies. A just energy transition for sustainable development.* Development Bank of the Latin America and the Caribbean.

Cardoso, F. H. (1972). Dependency and development in Latin America. *New Left Review, 74*(1), 83–95.

Claver-Carone, M. (2024). Making the Americas grow again. *Americas Quarterly, 3,* 29–35. https://www.americasquarterly.org/article/trumps-vision-make-the-americas-grow-again/

Crabtree, J. (2024). The fiction of western unity on China de-risking. *Foreing Affairs.* https://foreignpolicy.com/2024/12/05/trump-China-trade-tariffs-decoupling-derisking-europe-eu-allies/

de Graaf, T., Kribbe, H., & van Middelar, L. (2024). *Energy diplomacy. Europe's new strategic mission. A report by the Brussel Institute of Geopolitics.* Brussel Institute for Geopolitics.

de la Mora, L. M. (2023). The perpetual pursuit of integration in Latin America and the Caribbean. *CEPAL Review, 141,* 103–119. https://www.cepal.org/en/publications/69198-perpetual-pursuit-integration-latin-america-and-caribbean

Deberdt, R., DiCarlo, J., & Park, H. (2024). Standardizing "green" extractivism: Chinese & Western environmental, social, and governance instruments in the critical mineral sector. *The Extractive Industries and Society, 19,* 101516, 1–11. https://doi.org/10.1016/j.exis.2024.101516

Domínguez, R. (2023). China y su proyecto de reglobalización: de la *Belt and Road Initiative* a las iniciativas globales de desarrollo y seguridad. In R. Domínguez, & G. Lo Brutto (coords.), *La cooperación internacional en la encrucijada: Reglobalización versus órdenes mundiales solapados* (pp. 16–69). BUAP & Editorial Universidad de Cantabria.

Draghi, M. (2024). *The future of European competitiveness. Part A. A competitiveness strategy for Europe. Part B. In-depth analysis and recommendations.* European Commission.

Dussel Peters, P. (2024). *Monitor de la OFDI China en América Latina y el Caribe 2024.* Red ALC-China.

ECLAC. (2024a). *Foreign direct investment in Latin America and the Caribbean, 2024.* Economic Commission of Latin America and the Caribbean.

ECLAC. (2024b). Critical minerals for the energy transition and electromobility: Economic development opportunities and socioenvironmental challenges. *Natural Resources in the Latin America and the Caribbean, 6.* https://www.cepal.org/en/insights/critical-minerals-energy-transition-and-electromobility-economic-developmnt-opportunities

ECLAC (2024c). Natural resources outlook in Latin America and the Caribbean, 2023. Economic Commission for Latin America and the Caribbean.

Enfu, C., & Xia, L. (2024). Building a community with a shared future for humanity through China's six global initiatives. *International Critical Thought, 14*(2), 157–175. https://doi.org/10.1080/21598282.2024.2366560

European Commission. (2023). *Commission presents global gateway investment agenda with Latin American and the Caribbean.* Press release. https://ec.europa.eu/commission/presscorner/api/files/document/print/en/ip_23_3863/IP_23_3863_EN.pdf

European Commission. (2024). *A new agenda for relations between the EU and Latin America and the Caribbean.* Brussels, 7.6.2023. JOIN (2023) 17 final.

Fernández, V. R., González, J., & Merino, G. E. (2023). Latin America and China's belt and road initiative: Challenges and proposals forma ta Latin American perspective. *Austral: Brazilian Journal of Strategy & International Relations, 12*(23), 105–134.

Fortín, C., Heine, J., & Ominami, C. (2020). *El no alineamiento activo: un camino para Ameríca Latina y el Caribe.* Nueva Sociedad. https://nuso.org/articulo/el-no-alineamiento-activo-una-camino-para-america-latina/

Fortín, C., Heine, J., & Ominami, C. (2023). Conclusions. Implications of an Active Non-Alignment (ANA). In C. Fortín, J. Heine, & C. Ominami (Eds.), *Latin American foreign policies in the new world order* (pp. 263–273). Athem Press.

Granada, I., et al. (2022). *Atlas de Infraestructuras de integración de América Latina y el Caribe. Mapeando infraestructuras de transporte y logística de alto impacto en las cadenas de valor regionales.* Banco Interamericano de Desarrollo. https://doi.org/10.18235/0004538

Hendrik, C. (2023). *Why the proposed Brussels buyers club to procure critical minerals in a bad idea.* PIIE Policy Brief, Peterson Institute for International Economics.

Hirst, M., et al. (2024). América Latina y el Sur Global en tiempos sin hegemonías. *Revista CIDOB d'Afers Internacionals, 136*, 133–156. https://doi.org/10.24241/rcai.2024.136.1.133

Ishmael, L. (2024). *The new south: Breaking with the past: West-South engagement in a changing world* (IDOS discussion paper, 9/2024). https://doi.org/10.23661/idp9.2024

Jaguaribe, H. (1979). (1979). Autonomía periférica y hegemonía céntrica. *Estudios Internacionales, 12*(46), 91–130.

Johnson, C.A. et al. (2024). Bringing the state back in the lithium triangle: An institutional analysis of resource nationalism in Chile, Argentina, and Bolivia. *The Extractive Industries and Society, 20*, 101534, 1–12. https://doi.org/10.1016/j.exis.2024.101534

Katz, C. (2024). The new geopolitical scene in Latin America. In G. Albo (Ed.), *A new global geometry? Socialist register 2024* (pp. 247–260). The Merlin Press, Monthly Review Press and Fernwood Publishing.

Lebdioui, A. (2024). *Survival of the greenest. Economic transformation in a climate-conscious world.* UNU-Wider & Cambridge University Press. https://doi.org/10.1017/9781009339414

Lewis, W. A. (1950). The industrialization of the British West Indies. *Caribbean Economic Review, 2*(1), 1–61.

Lewis, W. A. (1978 [2010]). *Growth and fluctuations 1870–1913.* Routledge.

Lewkowicz, J. (2024). *Beyond the belt and road? What's next for the EU in Latin America.* https://dialogue.earth/en/business/beyond-the-belt-and-road-whats-next-for-the-eu-in-latin-america/

Ling, S. (2024). Can lithium OPEC be realized? Analysis of South America's lithium cartel. *Ibero-América Studies, 8*(2), 65–75. https://doi.org/10.55704/ias.v8i2.06

Martins, H. H. (2024). Rare earth geopolitics: Global dynamics and strategic balance of power. *Janus.net. E-journal of International Relations, 15*(1), 249–265.

MEE. (2024). *BRI Green Development Outlook.* Ministry of Ecology and Environment of the People's Republic of China, BRI International Green Development Coalition.

Milanez, B., & Dorn, F. M. (2024). Lithium policies in Latin America: Old wine in new bottles? *Extractivism Policy Brief, 8.* https://doi.org/10.17170/kobra-2024082710725

Morales, D. (2024a). El Foro China-CELAC a 10 años de su creación. *Latinoamérica21.* https://latinoamerica21.com/es/el-foro-china-celac-a-10-anos-de-su-creacion/

Morales, D. (2024b). El inicio de una nueva fase de las relaciones entre América Latina y China. *Latinomérica21.* https://latinoamerica21.com/es/el-inicio-de-una-nueva-fase-en-las-relaciones-entre-america-latina-y-china/

Müller, B., Ghiotto, L., & Bárcena, L. (2024). *The raw materials rush. How the European Union is using trade agreements to secure supply of critical raw materials for its green transition*. Transnational Institute.

Norton, B. (2024). *BRICS grows, adding 13 new "partner countries" at historic summit in Kazan, Russia*. https://geopoliticaleconomy.com/2024/10/26/brics-13-partner-countries-summit-kazan-russia/

Oglietti, M., et al. (2023). Moneda común y la nueva arquitectura financiera regional. https://www.sinpermiso.info/textos/moneda-comun-y-la-nueva-arquitectura-financiera-regional.

Olivera, M. (2019). Chapter 7: The possibilities of industrialization and structural change for the periphery in the context of globalization. In V. R. Fernández & G. Brondino (Eds.), *Development in Latin America. Critical discussions from the periphery*. https://doi.org/10.1007/978-3-319-92183-9_7

Overland, I. et al. (2019). The GeGaLo index: Geopolitical gains and losses after energy transition. *Energy Strategy Reviews, 26*, 100406, 1–16. https://doi.org/10.1016/j.esr.2019.100406

Panitch, L., & Gindin, S. (2012). *The making of global capitalism. The political economy of American Empire*. Verso.

Pérez Caldentey, E., & Verenengo, M. (2021). Financialization, premature deindustrialization, and instability in Latin America. *Review of Keynesian Economics, 9*(4), 493–511. https://doi.org/10.4337/roke.2021.04.03.

Ray, R., Albright, Z. C., & Dussel Peters, E. (2024). *China-Latin America and the Caribbean economic bulletin* (2024th ed.). Global Development Policy Center.

Ren, H. (2024). *Promoting international cooperation in industrial and supply chains*. https://en.cisce.org.cn/content/details1051_3702.html

Romero, C. A. et al. (2025). Trump y América Latina y el Caribe: ¿un laboratorio de control? *Nueva Sociedad*. https://nuso.org/documento/trump-y-america-latina-y-el-caribe-un-laboratorio-de-control/

Rosales, O. (2023). Latin America, The COVID-19 pandemic, and the restructuring of value chains. In C. Fortín, J. Heine, & C. Ominami (Eds.), *Latin American foreign policies in the new world order* (pp. 183–199). Athem Press.

Rubiolo, F., & Fiori, G. (2024). Litio, integración y sostenibilidad. Desafíos y oportunidades para la cooperación entre Argentina, Bolivia y Chile. In *Nuevas perspectivas de integración, cooperación y multilateralismo para América del Sur* (pp. 185–2014). CLACSO.

Sachs, J. (2024). Beyond hegemony. A new international order under the UN Charter. *Horizons: Journal of International Relations and Sustainable Development, 27*, 12–27. https://www.jstor.org/stable/e48517237

Scheneider, B. R. (1999). The *Desarrollista* State in Brazil and Mexico. In M. Woo-Cumings (Ed.), *The developmental state* (pp. 276–305). Cornell University Press.

Schindler, S., et al. (2024). The Second Cold War: US-China competition for centrality in infrastructure, digital, production, and finance networks. *Geopolitics, 29*(4), 1083–1120. https://doi.org/10.1080/14650045.2023.2253432

SEI et al. (2023). *The production gap: Phasing down or phasing up? Top fossil fuel producers plan even more extraction despite climate promises.* Stockholm Environmental Institute, Climate Analytics, E3G, International Institute for Sustainable Development and UNEP.

Stanley, L. E. (2020). *Latin America global insertion, energy transition, and sustainable development.* Cambridge University Press. https://doi.org/10.1017/9781108893398

Tagliapietra, S. (2024). The European Union's global gateway: An institutional and economic overview. *The World Economy, 47*(4), 1326–1335. https://doi.org/10.1111/twec.13551

Tran, H. (2024a). *How can the global south navigate geopolitical rivalry and geoeconomic fragmentation?* Policy Center for the New South Policy Brief, 07/2024.

Tran, H. (2024b). *The geopolitics of energy transition: Opportunities for the global south.* Policy Center for the New South Policy Brief, 65/2024.

Tran, H. (2025). *2025: Year of the middle powers.* Policy Center for the New South *Policy Brief*, 05/2025.

Tröster, B. Papatheophilou, S. and Küblböck, K. (2024). *In search of critical raw materials: What will the EU critical raw materials act achieve? An analysis of legal and factual implications of the CRMA.* OFSE Research Report, 17/2024.

Vadell, J., & Jabbour, E. (2024). Chinese embedded globalization: Social-economic formations in dispute in world reordering. *Globalizations, 21*(5), 931–949. https://doi.org/10.1080/14747731.2024.2302197

Vernengo, M. (2006). Technology, finance, and dependency: Latin American radical political economy in retrospect. *Review of Radical Political Economics, 38*(4), 551–568. https://doi.org/10.1177/0486613406293220

Victor, D. G., Roche, J., & Saraiva, J. (2024, April). *Energy transition and geopolitics: Are critical minerals the new oil?* World Economic Forum White Paper.

Vivoda, V. (2023). Friend-shoring and critical minerals: Exploring the role of the minerals security partnership. *Energy Research & Social Science, 100,* 103085, 1–7. https://doi.org/10.1016/j.erss.2023.103085

Vivoda, V., Matthews, R., & McGregor, N. (2024). A critical minerals perspective on the emergence of geopolitical trade blocs. *Resources Policy, 89*(104587), 1–9. https://doi.org/10.1016/j.resourpol.2023.104587

Wallerstein, I. (1974). Dependence in an interdependent world: The limited possibilities of transformation within the capitalist world economy. *African Studies Review, 17*(1), 1–26. https://www.jstor.org/stable/523574

Wang, Y. (2024). *Riding the trend of the times with a strong sense of responsibility.* Address by H.E. Wang Yi at the Symposium on the International Situation and China's Foreign Relations. https://www.mfa.gov.cn/eng/wjbzhd/202412/t20241217_11542540.html

Xi, J. (2024). *Working together for a fair and equitable global governance system.* Remarks by H.E. Xi Jinping at the Session II of the 19th G20 Summit. https://www.mfa.gov.cn/eng/xw/zyxw/202411/t20241119_11528781.html

Yang, Y., Xia, S., & Quian, X. (2023). Geopolitics of the energy transition. *Journal of Geographical Sciences, 33*(4), 683–704. https://doi.org/10.1007/s11442-023-2101-2

Yiping, H. (2024). Can China lead the global energy transition? *East Asia Forum.* https://doi.org/10.59425/eabc.1734904800

Zelikovich, J., & Yamin, P. (2024). Carrots or sticks? Analyzing the application of US statecraft towards Latin American engagement with China. *Latin American Politics and Society, 66*(4), 58–77. https://doi.org/10.1017/lap.2024.9

Zhao, M. (2024). The belt & road initiative and U.S.-China competition over the global South. *China Economic Journal, 17*(2), 166–181. https://doi.org/10.1080/17538963.2024.2344270

Zhou, G. (2024). Rise of Global South and changes in contemporary international order. *China International Strategy Review, 6*(1), 58–77. https://doi.org/10.1007/s42533-024-00160-x

Zhu, A. L. et al. (2024). China's nature-based solutions in the global south: Evidence from Asia, Africa, and Latin America. *Global Environmental Change, 86*, 102842, 1–13. https://doi.org/10.1016/j.gloenvcha.2024.102842

CHAPTER 6

Conclusions

Eva Paus and Rafael Domínguez

Abstract The book addresses two key questions in Latin America's development: how to use abundant natural resources for inclusive green development (IGD), and whether the global green transition can help move away from extractivism. The authors propose a strategy driven by a green developmental state and broadly conceptualized industrial policies. They argue that dependent IGD is possible if progressive governments provide strong leadership, build supportive coalitions, and embrace regional integration and strategic non-alignment. While constraints are significant (e.g., trade rules and limited fiscal space), national reforms and regional cooperation are essential. The IGD path requires leveraging critical mineral demand, strengthening small and medium enterprises, and balancing productivity, inclusion, and sustainability. However, political will, institutional capacity, and overcoming vested interests are crucial. Success also hinges on tailored national strategies reflecting diverse country contexts. Ultimately, only transformative governance—not business as usual—can steer resource-rich Latin American countries toward sustainable, equitable, and green development.

Keywords Inclusive green development • Natural resources • Green transition • Extractivism • Green developmental state • Industrial policies • Structural change • Regional integration • Political leadership • Critical minerals • Latin America

E. Paus, R. Domínguez, *Toward Inclusive Development in Latin America*, Palgrave Studies in Latin American Heterodox Economics, https://doi.org/10.1007/978-3-032-08588-7_6

A crisis is an opportunity riding a dangerous wind.
—Chinese proverb

We started this book with two questions which engage the enduring Latin American debate in the dependency research program: (1) How can the abundance in natural resources be transformed to support inclusive green development (IGD), and (2) Will it be possible to take advantage of the global green transition to break away from extractivism by leveraging the very wealth of natural resources?

In answer to the first question we propose a development strategy where a green developmental state is the driver, and broadly defined industrial policies (IPs) are at the core. Based on an approach of international political economy of structural change, our answer to the second question is cautiously and conditionally affirmative. There is a possibility for dependent development if progressive governments combine transformative leadership with the support of development-oriented coalitions to overcome key constraints at the national and international level, and if they use the current moment of extreme geopolitical uncertainty for strategic non-alignment and greater integration at the regional level.

The global green transition offers an opportunity for the resource-rich Latin American countries (RR-LAC) to leverage their natural resources for a move toward productivity-enhancing structural change, social inclusion, and green growth. And the renewed legitimacy of IPs in the Global North makes it easier for RR-LAC to embrace and pursue them. Unquestionably, the obstacles to IGD are considerable, especially when the future of the global economic and political architecture is shrouded in uncertainty. However, there is no pro-development alternative to systemic change toward IGD. After four decades of neoliberal policies with severe consequences (premature de-industrialization, re-primarization of exports and subordinated integration into global value chains, unresolved structural heterogeneity, persistence of income and wealth inequality, rampant informality, and widespread polarization), Hirschman's *fracasomania* or market-led strategies are simply not an option. Yet, if business as usual prevails, they are the default, and development challenges will continue to intensify.

To capitalize on the opportunity presented by the growing demand for critical minerals of the RR-LAC, we emphasize the vital importance of government leadership with a developmental-environmental mindset in adopting and implementing IPs as part of an IGD strategy. If political will and national leadership align, there are possibilities for leveraging the synergies among the three objectives of enhancing productivity, social inclusion, and energy transition.

If government leadership committed to an IGD agenda and sufficiently broad-based agreement on IPs are missing, other factors (capabilities, continuity, transparency, win-win polices, and a persuasive narrative) will not compensate, However, even with strong and transformative political leadership and a cohesive industrial strategy, new activities of dynamic comparative advantage are unlikely to generate sufficient decent employment opportunities given rapid technological change and the need to compete on productivity, not low wages. Therefore, it is essential for progressive governments to design complementary policies that focus on improving conditions for small and medium-sized enterprises, informal sector workers, and non-tradable services, to ensure that the benefits of development are distributed more equitably and sustainably over time and space.

Key factors constraining the policy and fiscal space for IGD are international trade and investment agreements (WTO disciplines and the investor-state dispute settlement mechanism) as well as limited financial resources. Actions at the international and national level are needed to broaden the space. Internationally, rules must align with the Sustainable Development Goals of the UN Agenda 2030 to support an IGD transition; and financial resources for this transition must be increased significantly. Nationally, governments can raise fiscal revenue by capturing a larger share of the natural resource rents, making the tax structure more progressive, and reducing tax evasion and avoidance. And they can expand policy space by terminating international investment agreements that include investor-state dispute settlement mechanisms, following the example of Ecuador and Bolivia.

Since international reforms are slow and uncertain, especially in light of the nationalist orientation of the second Trump Administration, the primary focus has to be on national and regional reforms. Governments should reassess the benefits of bilateral trade and investment treaties. For example, public procurement policies, which are generally prohibited, constitute important measures to create domestic markets for new products. At the regional level, coalitions of progressive governments with shared agendas are likely to be more effective than initiatives encompassing all CELAC members without shared political will.

International cooperation among like-minded Latin American countries working in a coordinated strategy of non-alignment is more important than ever. More cooperation and regional integration among Latin American governments would strengthen their ability to navigate the turbulent waters of strategic competition between the US and China, with the EU as a possible balancing factor. To prevent the repetition of a commodity trap (the reproduction of the unequal exchange model between those who control capital and technology and reap the benefits and those who possess natural resources and bear the social and environmental costs), like-minded countries must coordinate with each other and deepen their cooperation based on what works (tax cooperation, Escazú Agreement, coordination on renewables energies, integration of human capital, research networks in science and technology, transport infrastructure and logistics).

Political support at the national level and relative policy independence internationally are critical for the adoption and implementation of an IGD agenda. On the domestic front, there are several factors that potentially translate into electoral support for an IGD agenda: social stratification biased against lower-income segments, rising and unfulfilled expectations of public services, relatively young demographics, and strong concern about interpersonal and intergenerational inequalities. On the other hand, there are forces which make support for an IGD transition more fragile than expected: social contradictions generated by increasing vulnerability and a large informal economy, as well as the political dynamics influenced by tax deals, poor-quality public services, and high concern about inflation and insecurity.

In the context of soft and semi-patrimonial Latin American states and low-intensity and unequal democracies, progressive governments must resolve the contradiction between the logic of capital accumulation for IGD and the logic of interlinking social inequalities. They must strengthen their ties with development-oriented coalitions through institutionalized processes of dialogue and participation, including those at the bottom (social movements) and those at the top (fractions of the elite). The road ahead must be to move from social redistribution bargains (using the rents of extraction for poverty reduction, as in the first Pink Tide in Venezuela, Ecuador, or Bolivia) to bargains by a green developmental state with a focus on IGD for green growth and productivity-enhancing structural change, as sought currently in Uruguay and Chile.

On the external front, the structuralist dependency approach merged with world-systems analysis through the concept of development by invitation underscores the possibility of agency for national governments to pursue a strategy of dependent IGD. RR-LAC rely significantly on core countries (the US and EU) and a semi-peripheral country in transition to the core (China) to drive their process of structural transformation. Nonetheless, we suggest that the possibility for multiple games between the region and those three major actors through partnerships, coalitions or initiatives offers a window of opportunity to achieve IGD transformation. Governments face a delicate balancing act in the current global context, where Trump's tariffs and threats against taking sides with China coincide with Chinese rhetoric of win-win cooperation and a likely surge of their exports to Latin America (and other non-US destinations).

Throughout the book, we have emphasized the heterogeneity among RR-LAC notwithstanding key structural characteristics. The gravity of the three major economic challenges (productivity-enhancing structural change, social inclusion, energy transition) varies across countries. Accordingly, policy priorities cannot be the same either. Possibilities for change differ with state capacities, social capital, levels of inequality and informality, pragmatic leadership, governments' ability to muster sufficiently broad supportive coalitions, and their willingness and skill to loosen the considerable external and internal constraints in policy and fiscal realms.

Table 6.1 summarizes strengths RR-LAC have with respect to some of the main factors shaping the possibility of IGD that we discussed in the book. Although some countries clearly have more strengths than others, each country has some particular strength which it can leverage moving forward. However, there are key elements the table does not capture: importantly, the relative strength of vested interests in the current model on the one hand and of possible coalitions in support of an IGD strategy on the other.

We live in times of radical uncertainty as well as urgent need for a strategy which addresses LAC's key challenges. History shows that crisis is a moment of opportunity. However, the opportunity can be seized by a government doubling down on business as usual or one that offers a real alternative. Only the latter will put RR-LACs on the path to IGD.

Table 6.1 Selected strength factors for IGD in RR-LAC

	ARG	*BOL*	*BRA*	*CHI*	*COL*	*ECU*	*MEX*	*PAR*	*PER*	*URU*	*VEN*
Advantages in green transition											
Large proven reserves of critical minerals	X	X	X	X	X		X		X		
Net fossil fuel importers	X	X		X			X	X	X	X	X
Initial carbon tax	X			X	X						
Fiscal and policy space											
Few constraints from IIAs with ISDS		X	X			X					
Relatively high tax revenue/GDP	X		X							X	
Significant space for increasing government share of natural resource rents			X	X					X		
High share of fossil fuel subsidies in GDP	X	X				X	X				
IGD implementation											
Relatively high state capacity	X			X						X	
Relatively high trust in institutions				X						X	

(*continued*)

Table 6.1 (continued)

	ARG	*BOL*	*BRA*	*CHI*	*COL*	*ECU*	*MEX*	*PAR*	*PER*	*URU*	*VEN*
Relatively high increase in concern over income distribution during last decade	X				X						X
Relatively high willingness to mobilize for better health, safety, and equality		X	X					X	X		
Economic and financial issues are most important problems	X				X		X				X
Second pink tide		X	X	X	X		X				X

Source: Analysis in Chaps. 2, 3, 4, and 5

Correction to: Toward Inclusive Green Development in Latin America

Eva Paus and Rafael Domínguez

Correction to:
Chapter 1 in: E. Paus, R. Domínguez, *Toward Inclusive Development in Latin America*, Palgrave Studies in Latin American Heterodox Economics, https://doi.org/10.1007/978-3-032-08588-7_1

The book initially published with an incomplete version of table 1.2. This has been amended.

The updated version of this chapter can be found at https://doi.org/10.1007/978-3-032-08588-7_1

E. Paus, R. Domínguez, *Toward Inclusive Development in Latin America*, Palgrave Studies in Latin American Heterodox Economics, https://doi.org/10.1007/978-3-032-08588-7_7

Index[1]

[1] Note: Page numbers followed by 'n' refer to notes.

E. Paus, R. Domínguez, *Toward Inclusive Development in Latin America*, Palgrave Studies in Latin American Heterodox Economics, https://doi.org/10.1007/978-3-032-08588-7

G

H

I

T

U

FSC
www.fsc.org
MIX
Papier | Fördert gute Waldnutzung
FSC® C083411

Kolibri 360 GmbH
Ferdinand-Jühlke-Straße 7
99095 Erfurt, Deutschland
produktsicherheit@kolibri360.de